collector's g

LUNCHBOXES

METAL * VINYL * PLASTIC
IDENTIFICATION & VALUES

Carole Bess White & L. M. White

COLLECTOR BOOKS
A Division of Schroeder Publishing Co., Inc.

The current values in this book should be used only as a guide. They are not intended to set prices, which vary from one section of the country to another. Auction prices as well as dealer prices vary greatly and are affected by condition as well as demand. Neither the authors nor the publisher assumes responsibility for any losses that might be incurred as a result of consulting this guide.

Front cover: A-Team, $75.00, pg. 19; Snoopy w/blue cup, $300.00, pg. 196; Home Town Airport, $1,500.00, pg. 113; Ziggy's Munch Box, $150.00, pg. 279; Robin Hood, $225.00, pg. 181.

Back cover: Jetsons The Movie, $15.00, pg. 288; Underdog, $2,000.00, pg. 278.

Cover design by Beth Summers
Book design by Mary Ann Hudson

Searching For A Publisher?

We are always looking for knowledgeable people considered to be experts within their fields. If you feel that there is a real need for a book on your collectible subject and have a large comprehensive collection, contact Collector Books.

COLLECTOR BOOKS
P.O. Box 3009
Paducah, Kentucky 42002-3009

www.collectorbooks.com

Copyright © 2001 Carole Bess White & L.M. White

CONTENTS

DEDICATION

To all "boxers" who love, collect, and study lunchboxes, this book is respectfully dedicated.

ACKNOWLEDGMENTS

Heartfelt thanks to all of the families who gave so generously of their time, knowledge, and advice, and access to their collections.

Rob, Sam & Zeke Bender and Kristin Shetler:
Rob is a serious boxer and Internet dealer and is employed in the movie advertising industry.

Linda, Lyle & Brock Blow:
Linda's collection includes the tobacco tins shown on page 5.

Bill, Nancy, John, and Lizzie Brewer:
Collectors of a little bit of everything, they are the owners of many of the retro boxes on pages 11 and 12.

Fred & Jan Carlson:
Fred is one of America's foremost boxers, with a collection as large as it is legendary.

Dave Coons:
Dave is a member of Portland's Rain of Glass, a collector and dealer who always has just the right thing to be photographed for a book.

Dick & Sharon Pollard:
Dick has owned almost every metal box and bottle made from the 1950s to the 1990s. He maintains a sizeable collection of metals and vinyls, and a very high quality collection of thermos bottles. He also collects novelty telephones, picture discs, tin litho toys, board games, and children's books, and he has one of the largest collections of novelty transistor radios in the world. Dick is retired now and is interested in finding good homes for his "toys."

Linda & Sam Steward:
New to the collecting world, Linda contributed a retro box.

Sharon & Fred Wiley:
Sharon is a nurse, and in her "spare" time she has put together an amazing lunchbox collection.

Greg, Susan & Sean Wright:
Greg maintains a collection of high quality metal and vinyl lunch kits, and he is also an Internet dealer. In his "other" life, he works for a local school district.

Want to share information or ask questions? E-mail: cbessw@aol.com

Food containers have been around since people first walked the earth — leaves, gourds, animal skins, or whatever else was at hand. As we learned to use tools, our containers grew more sophisticated, until finally, the lunchbox was born. It started life as any sort of wooden, leather, cloth, wicker or tin container adapted for that use, and by the Victorian Age grew more specific.

The first patents for tin cans were obtained in England in 1810, and in the United States in 1825. In addition to canned perishable food, tins were also created for tobacco, candy, and cookies (called biscuits in England.) After the goodies were gone, the empty tins were perfect for carrying lunches.

Can manufacturers spotted a hole in the market and filled it with boxes specifically designed for lunches. When the thermos bottle was invented in 1903, the foundation was laid for the complete lunch kit.

**Dixie Queen Plug Cut Tobacco
Tin Lunchbox
by Tindeco**

**Tiger Chewing Tobacco
Tin Lunchbox**

**Union Leader Cut Plug Tobacco
Tin Lunchbox**

LUNCHBOX & THERMOS BOTTLE TIMELINE

By Carole Bess White and Dick Pollard

1892: **England**; vacuum bottle perfected by English scientist James Dewar

1902: **USA**; earliest known tin lithographed lunchbox in the shape of a small picnic basket

1903: **Germany**; first "Dewar Flask" vacuum bottle patented

1904: **Germany**; the name "Thermos," (from *therme*, Greek for heat) was selected for the vacuum bottle in a newspaper contest.

1906: **USA**; first known thermos bottle imported from Germany.

Production in the United States

1907: American Thermos Bottle Company patented the first thermos bottle in the United States.

1908: Mantle Lamp Company of America began making kerosene lamps with metal fittings under the trade name Aladdin.

1911: American Thermos Bottle Company made their first workman's lunch kit (box and Thermos bottle).

1920: American Thermos Bottle Company made their first child's lunch kit.

1931: Ohio Art entered the lunchbox market with their "Sports" and "Transportation" carry-all lunch pails without thermos bottles

1930s: Decoware began manufacturing tin lunch pails, mainly carry-alls with two handles.

1935: **First known licensed character lunch pail:** Geuder, Paeschke & Frey Company manufactured the first licensed character lunch pail, Mickey Mouse.

1940s: American Thermos Bottle Company made its first undecorated metal boxes.

1945: The benchmark year when steel became widely available and lunchbox manufacturers were able to convert entirely to steel.

1946: Aladdin Industries (formerly the Mantle Lamp Company) began selling undecorated steel lunch kits in red and blue enamel, with thermos bottles.

1950: **First licensed T.V character kit ever made:** Aladdin Industries began producing Hopalong Cassidy lunch kits. The box was red or blue enameled steel; it had an oval decal of Hoppy with "scalloped" edges, and a matching lithographed bottle.

1950: Aladdin Industries moved from Chicago to Nashville.

1953: **First four-color lithographed steel TV character lunch kit:** American Thermos Bottle Company entered the TV character lunch box market with their first fully lithographed box, Roy Rogers, and a matching lithographed bottle.

1954: Aladdin Industries entered the lithographed box market with Hopalong Cassidy, and Tom Corbett Space Cadet.

1954: Adco Liberty made their first fully lithographed lunch kit, Lone Ranger.

1954: Landers, Frary & Clark manufactured their first fully lithographed lunch kit, Superman (under the Universal trademark).

1956: Adco Liberty quit the lunch kit business after a dispute with Walt Disney Enterprises. Their offense was putting Kit Carson, a non-Disney character, on the other side of a Disney Davy Crockett box.

1956: Disney licensed Aladdin Industries to make its character lunchboxes.

1957: **First lithographed dome kits were made:** Buccaneer by Aladdin Industries, and Red Barn by American Thermos Bottle Company.

1957: Ohio Art manufactured their first of many standard (rectangular) steel boxes, Frontier Days and Sports Afield; all were made without matching bottles.

1957: Plastic handles were first used by American Thermos Bottle Company.

1958: Ohio Art produced its last carry-all lunch pail.

1959: **First vinyl boxes produced:** Aladdin Industries, Bobby Soxer; American Thermos Bottle Company, Ponytails; Ardee, Generic (unlicensed art) Boxes; Universal, Pen Pals.

1960: King Seeley purchased the American Thermos Bottle Company and changed the name to the King Seely Thermos Company.

1962: **First embossed (three-dimensional) steel box made:** Huckleberry Hound by Aladdin Industries.

1962: **Brunch bags** (zippered vinyl bags with strap handles) introduced by Aladdin Industries.

1962: Ohio Art began using plastic handles.

1965: Landers, Frary & Clark (Universal) went out of business. General Electric's Housewares Division purchased the lunchbox and bottle dies, and the Universal trademark.

1965: Standard Plastic Products, the manufacturer of King Seeley Thermos Company's vinyl boxes, was purchased by the Mattel Toy Company and stopped producing boxes.

1965: King Seeley Thermos Company's first shortened bottles and first use of larger boxes.

1965 – 66: Air Flite produced Beatles vinyl lunchboxes with no bottles, their only known boxes.

1966 – 68: Spin Games, the first boxes with spin games by King Seeley Thermos Company.

1968 – 69: Aladdin Industries started using plastic bottles instead of the more expensive steel and glass ones.

1970s: Ardee Industries closed.

1972: **The beginning of the end:** King Seeley Thermos Company produced their first injection-molded plastic boxes. Legend has it that the state of Florida banned steel lunchboxes. Whether it was due to a ban or because steel boxes were more expensive to produce, other states and Canada followed over the next 10 years, forcing the switch to plastic boxes.

1972 – 73: King Seeley Thermos Company also started using plastic bottles and switched to plastic latches as well.

1973: Aladdin Industries produced a narrower plastic bottle but dropped it after a year.

1973: Aladdin Industries (Canada) produced plastic boxes.

1972: Okay Industries purchased the Landers, Frary & Clark equipment and Universal trademark from General Electric.

1973: Okay Industries produced its first steel lunch kits (identical in design to Universal kits, since they were made from the same equipment, but with different characters) with steel and glass bottles stamped Universal.

1974: Okay Industries switched to plain plastic bottles.

1977: King Seeley Thermos Company produced its first "Munchie Bag" and produced its last standard (flat, rectangular) vinyl boxes.

1978: Okay Industries discontinued lunch kit production.

1980: Aladdin Industries (America) joined the parade and started producing injection-molded plastic boxes.

1982: Aladdin Industries' last vinyl boxes, Sesame Street, Pink Panther & Annie.

1983: Aladdin Industries started producing standard (flat, rectangular) plastic boxes.

1985: Ohio Art discontinued steel boxes.

1986: Aladdin Industries discontinued steel boxes.

1987: **The end of an era:** King Seeley Thermos Company discontinued steel boxes; Rambo was the last one made by an American company.

Major Lunchbox Manufacturers

Adco Liberty, West Orange, New Jersey

Made steel lunchboxes from 1954 to 1956, including Davy Crockett, Howdy Doody, Lone Ranger, Mickey Mouse/Donald Duck, and Superman. They lost their Disney licensing in a dispute over including Kit Carson, a non-Disney character, on a Disney Daniel Boone box, and quit the lunch kit business.

Air Flite (probably New York)

Made vinyl Beatles lunchboxes during the 1960s.

Aladdin Industries, Chicago, Illinois, and Nashville, Tennessee

Known to glass collectors for its Aladdin and "Alacite" lamps, Aladdin Industries started in 1908 as the Mantle Lamp Company of America. They later assumed their trademark name and became Aladdin Industries. They produced steel, vinyl, and plastic lunchboxes.

American Thermos Bottle Company

Produced America's first thermos bottle in 1907. Manufactured steel and vinyl lunch kits and boxes under that name until 1960, when they were bought out and became King Seeley Thermos Company.

Ardee Industries, Hagerstown, Maryland

Manufactured vinyl lunch kits sold in discount chain stores such as Woolworth and K-Mart in the 1960s and 1970s. Most of them were plain, standard (rectangular) boxes with a clear vinyl pocket on the front for a lithographed paper sheet. Ardee manufactured between 10 and 15 million vinyl lunchboxes during its years in business.

Cheinco, Chein Industries, Burlington, New York

Manufactured line of small, lithographed steel "carry-all" lunch pails in the 1980s modeled on the carry-all pails of the 1930s – 1950s. Some of their pails included Return of the Jedi, Cracker Jack, Oreos, and Donald Duck. They did not include thermos bottles.

DecoWare

Manufactured oval or rectangular carry-all lunch pails in the 1930s and 1940s. The pails were tin, with two stamped tin handles, and usually had a pie tray insert.

Geuder, Paeschke and Frey, Milwaukee, Wisconsin

Manufactured a small, tin, oval Mickey Mouse lunch pail from 1935 to 1937 for Disney Enterprises.

General Steel Ware, Canada

Produced at least one known steel lunchbox in the 1960s, Sleeping Beauty.

King Seeley Thermos Company

Began life as American Thermos Bottle Company; in 1960 King Seeley bought out American Thermos and the name was changed to King Seeley Thermos Company. They sold lunch kits marked with various designs of the Thermos logo.

Kruger Manufacturing Company, Canada

Made one known steel lunchbox in 1955: Walt Disney Official Davy Crockett.

Landers, Frary & Clark

Manufactured lunchboxes and kits from 1954 to 1963 under the name Universal.

Libbey Glass Company

Produced Disney lunch pails from 1938 to 1941, including Snow White and Pinocchio.

Ohio Art

Produced steel lunchboxes (but not bottles) from 1931 to 1985. Before 1931, they were Spencer Bartlett & Co. They began producing carry-all lunch pails in 1931; they converted to standard (flat, rectangular) boxes in 1957, and stopped producing carry-alls by 1958.

Okay Industries

Purchased Landers, Frary & Clark's Universal lunchbox stamping equipment and part of their remaining stock of thermos bottles and began producing steel lunch kits in 1973. The first Okay kits, such as Action Jackson and Underdog, contained matching steel and glass character thermos bottles still stamped Universal. All perfectly legal — they bought the name and the dies lock, stock, and barrel. In 1974 Okay switched to plain plastic bottles. However, the Okay boxes look like the Universal boxes because they were made from the same equipment.

Omni Graphics
Made one known kit, the 1960s Volkswagen steel box and matching bottle.

Owens Illinois Can Company
Formed in 1936 when Libbey Glass Company absorbed three smaller can companies, including Tindeco. From 1938 to 1941, Libbey Glass produced Disney lunch pails including Snow White and Pinocchio. Owens Illinois ceased metal stamping entirely in 1945.

Spencer Bartlett & Company
Ohio Art Company's original name.

Standard Plastic Products
Made all of the Thermos vinyl lunch kits from 1959 to 1965, starting with the Ponytails series. Also made their own vinyl "Kaboodle Kits" line featuring the Beatles, Mickey Mouse, and Fess Parker.

Stanley Company
Made vacuum bottles from 1913 throughout the 1920s, when the company was purchased by Landers, Frary & Clark. Landers, Frary & Clark included a Stanley bottle in their line until they were purchased by General Electric in 1965. Aladdin bought the Stanley trademark and continued to sell Stanley bottles. Stanley bottles were not sold in children's lunch kits.

Tindeco
Originally part of the American Tobacco Company, Tindeco produced attractive, brightly colored lithographed tobacco, candy, and cookie tins in the 1920s and 1930s, including character tins such as Mother Goose, Peter Rabbit, and Santa Claus. While they were not actually produced as lunch pails, the resemblance is there. Libbey Glass Company absorbed Tindeco in 1936.

Universal
Trademark name of the Landers, Frary & Clark Company for the lunchboxes they produced from 1954 to 1963. As noted earlier, Okay Industries purchased LFC's lunchbox production equipment, including the Universal trademark and a significant portion of Universal's existing vacuum bottle stock.

Major Suppliers to Lunchbox Manufacturers

American Can Company, Brooklyn, New York, and Birmingham, Alabama
Produced steel lunchboxes for other companies. They made all American Thermos Bottle Company's steel boxes from the late 1940s until 1965. After that, they lithographed steel production sheets throughout the 1960s and 1970s for Aladdin Industries. Reputedly when steel boxes stopped being sold, American Can sold its remaining inventory of lithographed sheets including Paladin and The Jetsons to a scrap steel dealer to be used as roofing material in Pakistan.

Chicago Litho, Chicago, Illinois
Made the four-color lithographic press plates for Aladdin Industries from 1963 to 1986, and for King Seeley Thermos Company from 1974 to 1989.

Graphic Arts
Made the four-color lithographic press plates for American Thermos Bottle Company/King Seeley Thermos Company from 1953 to 1973. King Seeley Thermos Company was dissatisfied with the quality of Graphic Arts reproduction, and they switched to Chicago Litho in 1974.

Pittsburgh Metal Lithography
Made steel production sheets (which were then formed into lunchboxes) for Adco Liberty, King Seeley Thermos Company, Okay Industries, and Landers, Frary & Clark (Universal).

Plastene Corporation
American Thermos Bottle Company purchased the Plastene Corporation in 1952, which then produced all the plastic parts for their lunchboxes, such as handles, bottle stoppers, and cups. They produced King Seeley Thermos Company's plastic bottles and lunchboxes until they closed in 1989.

W.H. Hutchinson
Lithographed the steel production sheets for Aladdin in the 1960s and 1970s.

IT'S ABOUT TIME – THE PRESENT

Metal rules, but there are other contenders to the throne

The King: Older (1987 and earlier) steel lunchboxes and kits remain the popular favorites among collectors. Values have continued to rise, with no end in sight.

What will the next decade bring as Pre-Boomers and Baby Boomers, who comprise the largest and strongest market for metal boxes, begin to retire and divest themselves of their "stuff?" Will the market continue to rise, or will it flatten out like so many categories of collecting do as their buyers age out of the hobby? Only time will tell.

The Co-Regent: Vinyl boxes are coming up strong behind metal. Due to their fragility, vinyls present the greatest challenge to collectors. They were simply a vinyl sheath over a cardboard backing, and as such were often victims of the elements, or a bit of rough handling. One mother shared that it was not uncommon for her to have to purchase three or four different vinyls during the course of the school year. Each type of vinyl has its proponents: drawstring bags, brunch bags/munchies bags, and standard (flat rectangular) boxes. The scarcity of vinyls, their pleasing colors, and subject matters make them attractive to collectors, and prices are rising accordingly.

The Heir to the Throne: Watch your backs, metal and vinyl collectors, and keep salting away those plastic boxes! We all collect our childhood to one degree or another. As Netsters (formerly known as the "post-TV generation," born 1979 – 1984) turn nostalgic and begin to look for their childhood memories, plastic lunchboxes could well be on their lists. Right now most plastic kits are available for pretty close to their original retail prices — or even less, but a fortunate few have appreciated a bit better than that. So if you choose to invest, buy only absolutely mint ones, watch what you pay, and you just might be sitting on a stockpile of the Next Big Thing in the collecting world . . . or, maybe not! As always, "it's about time," and only time will tell.

Care and Cleaning

All collectors have their tried-and-true methods for cleaning boxes, from a damp cloth to chemicals. Less is more when it comes to box cleaning — it's always risky to clean too vigorously or harshly.

All the care and cleaning in the world are not going to turn damaged boxes into mint boxes, but sometimes they can be helped considerably.

If a box needs more than a wipe-down with a damp cloth, the first line of defense is warm, soapy water. Use a soft cloth, and dry the box thoroughly when you are finished, especially the metal clasps and hinges. Rust can damage hinges pretty quickly, so don't let it get started.

As the title of the Neil Young album says, "Rust Never Sleeps." Once started, rust will just keep on eating through your box unless stopped in its tracks. It will never heal, but storing your clean boxes in a warm, dry place will at least inhibit rust. Don't touch Naval Jelly-type rust removers to the painted surfaces boxes because they will damage the paint.

Some collectors like to clean and wax their boxes, but most wax yellows over time.

Tape will usually come off by scratching with your fingernail, but you may need to soak it in a bit of warm water first. If there is rust on the box, try using cotton balls soaked in warm water just on the taped area so you don't have to wet the rusted areas. Again, be very careful because even a fingernail can damage the paint.

Marking pen or other ink is a challenge. If it won't wash off with soap and water, test alcohol, nail polish remover (acetone,) turpentine or lighter fluid on a very small, unobtrusive area of the box with a Q-tip to see if the paint will discolor, then proceed with caution.

Dick Pollard suggests cautious use of Brasso for many cleaning chores.

IT'S ABOUT TIME – THE FUTURE

What will be hot in the 21st century?

Tiny lunchboxes, American Specialty Candy Confections, Inc., made in China.

Felix dome box, American Specialty Candy Confection, Inc., made in China.

Gone Fishing dome box, American Specialty Candy Confections, Inc., made in China.

Metals are back ... sort of

Merchandisers are no dummies when it comes to cashing in on a trend, and lunchboxes are no exception. Miniature metal lunchboxes both with and without candy or snack food, souvenir "collector" boxes for various entertainment entities, lunchboxes containing sports cards, and lunch-box-like containers meant to be used as handbags or mini briefcases have been sold in recent years. In fact, these boxes are meant for just about anything but lunch for small children. Many of them are imported from China. They don't have great value now — most retail for $4.00 – 20.00 — but, again, who knows what the future may hold.

What is a reproduction, a reissue, and a retro?

A *reproduction* is a new box made to look like an original old one by a company that did not issue it in the first place. See page 295 for several reproduction boxes.

A *reissue* is a new box made from old art that is owned by the original company or has been purchased by another company. The owner has a legal right to reissue whatever they think will sell in today's market, and they have no obligation to mark the new boxes any differently than the old.

A *retro* is a fantasy box, one that never was issued in the "old days," but looks like it could have or should have been. The boxes on this page and the Nickelodeon and Upper Deck boxes on page 12 are good examples of retro boxes.

We Can Do It! box.

TV Land, Nickelodeon, 1990s.

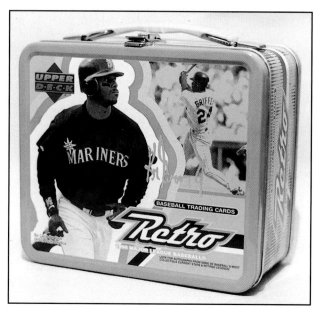

1998 Upper Deck Retro lunchbox sports card container.

How far will nostalgia take us?

If people collect their childhood, will the children's backpacks of today be their collectibles of tomorrow?

Batman Lunch Lugger
Thermos © 1991

LUNCHBOX ARTISTS

Victor Alongi:
Freelancer, designed many of KST's plastic kits.

Sally Augustini:
Bob Burton's assistant; worked on Aladdin's boxes for girls, such as Junior Miss.

Brenda Bassler:
Freelancer; designed Heathcliff & Pink Panther kits for Aladdin.

Mark Bellerose:
Designed the 1982 GI Joe kit for KST.

Jim Blackburn:
Freelancer; designed Archies kit & U.S. Mail dome box for Aladdin.

Wayne Boring:
Drew the Superman comic strip and designed the 1954 Superman box for Universal.

Charlie Brown:
Freelancer; contracted by Nick LoBianco to design boxes for KST such as Blondie and Bullwinkle, and to sketch boxes for other artists to finish, such as Popeye and Smokey the Bear.

Beverly Burge:
Succeeded Elmer Lehnhardt as Aladdin's art director; designed many kits for Aladdin, including Disney and Seasame Street.

Robert O. Burton:
Became art director for Aladdin in 1946; designed many of Aladdin's best kits including the first Hopalong Cassidy box. Also created the Kentucky Fried Chicken logo, and several Bob's Big Boy restaurant interiors and uniforms.

Milton Caniff:
Comic strip artist; drew the Steve Canyon strip and designed the box for Aladdin.

Sam Cohen;
Freelancer; designed Corsage and MacPherson Plaid kits for KST.

Ann Cummings:
1970s Aladdin staffer; designed many kits including Winnie the Pooh and Raggedy Ann & Andy.

Jack Davis:
Staff artist for DC Comics and MAD Magazine; designed The Man From U.N.C.L.E. kit for KST.

Jim Davis:
Created the Garfield comic strip; designed all KST's plastic Garfield boxes.

Disney Studios:
Thought to have provided art work for their boxes prior to 1957, when they began using Aladdin's artists.

Jess Hager:
Freelancer; designed Captain Astro and Bond XX for Ohio Art.

Don Henry:
KST artist in the 1970s, created Space Shuttle and Star Wars, among others.

John Henry:
Freelancer; designed several Aladdin kits including the Flintstones and Tarzan.

Dan Hosse:
Aladdin staffer in the 1980s, designed Thundercats.

Junior Miss, shown on page 123.

The Flintstones, shown on page 88.

Lunchbox Artists

Victor Johnson:
Son of Aladdin's owner had the big idea! His suggestion that a Hopalong Cassidy decal be placed on a lunchbox started lunch kits as we know them today.

Bob Jones:
Freelancer; created Aladdin's Dirt Bike, Grizzly Adams, and many more.

Al Konetzni:
Disney executive who had the original idea for the Disney school bus dome box, the most successful lunchbox of all time, selling more than 9,000,000 kits from 1961 – 1973.

William Kulman:
Freelancer; designed the Early West boxes for Ohio Art.

Elmer Lehnhardt:
Art director for Aladdin in the '60s and '70s; designed many kits including the Beatles and Land of the Giants (his self-portrait box).

Gene Lemery:
Freelancer; designed most of KST's kits from 1976 to 1986, including The A-Team, Knight Rider, and Mr. Merlin.

Rinaldo Leverone:
Designed KST's Hot Wheels kit.

Nick LoBianco:
Freelancer for KST; designed Get Smart, Julia, Yellow Submarine, and many more; in 1966 Charles Schulz turned over the marketing of the Peanuts characters to LoBianco who created the licensed Peanuts merchandise.

Jock Marshall:
Freelancer; created the Americana kit for American Thermos.

Bruce Matthews:
Freelancer; designed the Ronald McDonald/Sheriff of Cactus Canyon kit for Aladdin.

Milt Neil:
Designed the Howdy Doody kit for Adco Liberty.

T. Oughten:
Freelancer: contracted by Nick LoBianco as a finish artist for the KST Battle kit and Fess Parker/Daniel Boone kits.

Sam Petrucci:
Freelancer; designed the Magic of Lassie kit for KST.

John Polgreen:
Freelancer; designed KST's Astronaut dome box.

Bill Randolph:
Freelancer; designed Aladdin's 1977 Mickey Mouse Club kit.

Leo Schein:
Freelancer; designed several of KST's plastic kits in the 1980s.

Dee Wenner:
Freelancer; designed Sabrina and many of Aladdin's brunch bags in the 1970s.

Ed Wexler:
Staff illustrator for American Can Company; designed most of American Thermos's kits from 1953 – 1964, including Boating, Roy Rogers, and Hometown Airport.

Wally Wood:
Freelancer for several lunchbox manufacturers; designed Supercar for Universal, and finished Fireball XL5 for KST.

The Magic of Lassie, shown on page 138.

HOW LUNCHBOXES ARE MADE

Steel Lunchboxes

1. Steel was rolled into sheets then cut to size.

2. The sheets were printed with four-color illustrations by a printing process called lithography, and in some cases they were embossed (a pattern was stamped into them) as well.

3. The lithographed sheets were formed, or stamped, into the shape of the box and lid, whether standard (flat, rectangular), dome or carry-all.

4. Hinges, clasps, and handles were added as the boxes were assembled.

Vinyl Lunchboxes

1. Vinyl sheets are printed with illustrations (or in some cases, left plain) and cut to shape.

2. If the boxes carried clear vinyl sleeves, they were added at this point. The vinyl sheets were folded around cardboard backing, then heat sealed at the seams.

3. Hinges, clasps, and handles were added to standard (flat rectangular) boxes, drawstrings were added to the drawstring bags, or zippers and strap handles were added to brunch bags.

Plastic Lunchboxes

Plastic is extruded into sheets, decals or lithographed art is applied, and the boxes are shaped. Handles are added, and latches as well, if they are not built into the box, and voila, another box is born.

Thermos Bottles

Prior to 1969, thermos bottles consisted of a steel tube into which was screwed a glass liner, In 1969, Aladdin switched to round plastic bottles with glass liners, which still required assembly. Later, injection-molded round plastic and square plastic bottles became the industry standard. Also, molded styrofoam bottles were made all along, the least expensive to manufacture.

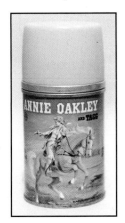

1955

1969

round plastic bottle

15

HOW TO USE THIS BOOK

Lunchboxes will be described in boxes like the example below. Keys to the manufacturer abbreviations and explanations of the rarity scale and condition scale follow.

Name of Box				
MFG	Date	Rarity	Type of box and value (Embossed boxes are noted as such, un-noted are flat)	Type of bottle & value

Box names beginning with numbers such as 18 Wheeler are in alphabetical, not numerical, order.
Note: Box names in quote marks are common names among collectors because the actual manufacturer's names are unknown.

Metal Box Manufacturers

AD: Adco Liberty
AL: Aladdin Industries
AT: American Thermos
Deco: Decoware
Cheinco: Cheinco
CC: Continental Can
GSW: General Steel Ware
KST: King Seeley Thermos Co.

K: Krueger
LIB: Libbey Glass Co.
N Y M: New York Metal Packaging
OA: Ohio Art
OK: Okay Industries
OG: Omni Graphics
UN: Universal Industries
UNK: Unknown

Rarity Scale

10
Very rare, only a few known

9-8
Very hard to find, very desirable

7-6
Moderately hard to find, also very desirable

5-4
Fairly common now, but getting harder to find

3-1
Very common, a good place to start your collection

Vinyl/Plastic Manufacturers

AD: Adco Liberty
AIR: Air Flite
AL: Aladdin Industries
AR: Ardee
AT: American Thermos
AV: Avon
BA: Babcock (Nappe Babcock)
BV: Bayville
CC: Continental Can
DA: Dart
DAS: D.A.S.
DCT: Deco Taiwan
DE: Deka
FD: Fun Design
FE: Feldco
FP: Fisher Price
FS: Fesco
FU: Fundes
GA: Gary
HB: Hasbro
HBT: Hanna Barbera, Taiwan

HU: Hummer
K: Kruger
KST: King Seeley Thermos
     In later years, only the THERMOS logo
     may appear on the box or bottle, but the
     company name is still KST
MK: Metrokane
NE: Neevel
OA: Ohio Art
OC: Outer Circle
OK: Okay Industries
PP: Prepac
SDT: Selandia Designs, Taiwan
SE: Servo
SPP: Standard Plastic Products
SU: Superseal
TR: Traffic
TU: Tupperware
UNK: Unknown
VBI: Volkswein Bros.
WDP: Walt Disney Productions

"Bicycle Riders", shown on page 33.
R: 9

Condition Scale for Metal Boxes

10+ (pristine)
Right out of the original shipping carton — never touched a store shelf; has original tags & stickers.

10 (mint)
Virtually brand new; no shelf wear or damage; desirable to have original tag and/or stickers; slick, smooth, and shiny, like a newly minted coin.

9 (near mint)
No rust; very light minor surface damage such as scratches or nicks; all surfaces look and feel wet to the touch.

8 (excellent)
No rust to speak of; light scratching; minor worn spots; light edge wear.

7 (fine)
Some rust spots; more rim wear and worn spots; small dents; surface feels dry.

6 (very good)
Heavier rust damage; rims more worn; larger dents; damaged latches or handles.

5 (good)
Heavy wear and dents on outside; rust inside.

4 (fair)
One good side only.

3 (poor)
Two very bad sides.

2 (terrible)
Faded, very heavy rust and dents on outside; rusted, worn and scratched on inside; missing handle or clasps.

1 (don't bother)
Surfaces rusted out or painted over; can't easily tell which box it is.

Relating Condition, Rarity, and Value

Most of the boxes pictured in this book are condition 8, 9, or 10. A few are 7, which are included because it seemed more important to show them than to hold out for perfection. However, condition is a very personal decision; an 8 to one collector may be a 7 to another. Many collectors use a fractional system for grading: 8¼, 8½, 8¾, etc. So, it's up to the buyer to decide what he can accept, until a better one comes along.

Values are given for condition 8 regardless of the appearance of the box in the picture, and they are meant to be a guide, based on in-person and Internet buying and selling.

Rarity is an important concern when making a buying decision. A rare box in condition 7, 6 or even lower might well be worth considering, while a more common box in that condition might better be declined because chances are good that a better example will come along soon.

While the final price is always determined by the buyer and seller, here are some things to remember:

The Internet

Oh those thrilling days of yesteryear ... many of us remember the "good old days" of garage sales, flea markets, shops, and shows when prices were low and lunch kits were plentiful.

In its own way, that's how the Internet is today. It is sort of like a giant garage sale and the finest antique store combined! Just like garage sales, there are bargains to be had — sometimes at a fraction of an item's true worth, but the really good stuff can go amazingly high.

Is the lowest Internet price the true value of an item? No — just like it wouldn't be if you found it at a garage sale. It's only the given price on a given day in a given auction. The next auction, or the next day, the price can be totally different. Internet auction prices are affected by the time of day the auction closes (who wants to stay up until 2:00 a.m. Pacific time anyway?) and the time of year, too.

When two or more buyers get auction fever, prices can spike astronomically. Does this make that inflated price the true worth of the box? Not necessarily! It may be just what a fevered few were willing to pay in the heat of the moment, the same as an in-person auction.

When an online auction closes, the price you see on the screen may or may not be the final price, depending on whether there is a reserve price on the item. The seller is free to set his reserve at whatever he chooses. If the reserve has not been met, the high bidder and seller are free to make a deal. The final price they arrive at is just between them, and you have no way of knowing how close the selling price is to the final bid on the screen.

The Internet is changing rapidly, too. As more and more people shop there, competition is increasing, and prices are rising constantly and may eventually level out just as flea market prices have done.

So get in while the getting's good if you've a mind to, but don't be surprised as the online market changes just as it has for in-person buying and selling.

Insuring Your Collection

If you get lucky and find a box for $10 that books for $100, what insurance value are you going to put on it? Exactly. In addition to being a guide to what the market will bear, book values are also a guide to *replacement* values.

Condition, Condition, Condition

One of the benefits of in-person buying is that you and you alone determine whether the condition is acceptable. On the Internet, you are taking an item on faith, and a purchase doesn't always work out the way you expect. That aside, prices in this book are for condition 8 boxes and bottles because 8 is the average condition.

Values for conditions 9, 10 or 10+ may be slightly higher than 8, or in many cases much higher, depending on rarity, desirability, and condition.

Values for condition 7 through 1 should be substantially lower than condition 8, so beware!

Here are a few examples of the conditions of lunchboxes you may find in your search.

Superman
condition 10+

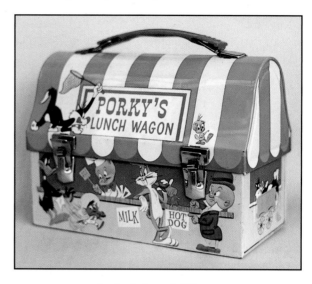

Porky's Lunch Wagon
condition 10

VW Bus
condition 9½ – 10

The Man from U.N.C.L.E.
condition 9 – 9½

The Green Hornet
condition 8½ – 9

Knight in Armor
condition 8 – 8½

STEEL LUNCH KITS, BOXES & BOTTLES

1. front

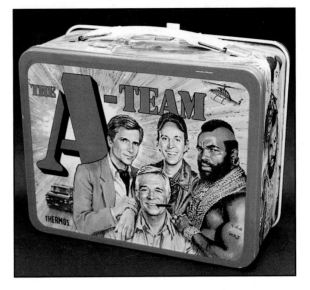

1. back

1. bottle

2. front & bottle

1. A-TEAM				
ARTIST: GENE LEMERY				
KST	1985	R: 5	STANDARD BOX $75	MATCHING SQUARE PLASTIC BOTTLE $35

2. ACTION JACKSON				
SAME FRONT & BACK				
OK	1973	R: 9	STANDARD BOX $700	MATCHING ROUND PLASTIC BOTTLE $450

3. front

3. back

3. ADDAMS FAMILY				
BASED ON THE HANNA-BARBERA CARTOON OF THE TV SITCOM; ARTIST: NICK LoBIANCO				
KST	1974	R: 5	STANDARD BOX $100	MATCHING SQUARE PLASTIC BOTTLE $35

4. front

4. back

4. AHIRU NO PEKKLE				
SANRIO, HAMBURG GERMANY, MADE IN KOREA	1994	R: 5	BOX $50	BOTTLE UNKNOWN

5. front

5. back

5. AIRLINE (NATIONAL AIRLINE)				
OA	1968	R: 6	STANDARD BOX $100	NO MATCHING BOTTLE MADE

6. front

6. back

6. AMERICA ON PARADE/WALT DISNEY ARTIST: BEVERLY BURGE				
AL	1976	R: 4	EMBOSSED STANDARD BOX $65	MATCHING ROUND PLASTIC BOTTLE $30

7. front & bottle

8. front

			7. AMERICANA ARTIST: JOCK MARSHALL	
AT	1958	R: 8	STANDARD BOX $375	MATCHING STEEL/GLASS BOTTLE $125

			8. ANIMAL FRIENDS/RED (SKY HAS BLUE & RED CLOUDS; SAME BACK & FRONT)	
OA	1978	R: 3	STANDARD BOX $50	NO MATCHING BOTTLE MADE

9. front

9. back

			9. ANNIE BASED ON THE MOVIE; ARTIST: BEVERLY BURGE	
AL	1981	R: 2	EMBOSSED STANDARD BOX $30	MATCHING ROUND PLASTIC BOTTLE $20

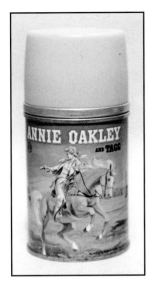

10. bottle

11. front

10. ANNIE OAKLEY & TAGG				
ARTIST: BOB BURTON				
AL	1955	R: 8	STANDARD BOX $375	MATCHING STEEL/GLASS BOTTLE $125

11. APPLE'S WAY				
BASED ON THE TV SERIES; ARTIST: NICK LoBIANCO				
KST	1975	R: 5	STANDARD BOX $90	MATCHING SQUARE PLASTIC BOTTLE $40

12. front

12. back

12. bottle

12. THE ARCHIES				
ARTIST: JIM BLACKBURN				
AL	1970 – 1971	R: 5	EMBOSSED STANDARD BOX $85	MATCHING ROUND PLASTIC BOTTLE $40

13. front

13. ASTRONAUT				
ARTIST: JOHN POLGREEN				
KST	1960	R: 7	DOME BOX $250	MATCHING STEEL/GLASS BOTTLE (SAME AS USED FOR SATELLITE) $80

13. back

13. bottle

14. front

14. back

14. THE ASTRONAUTS				
HONORING NEIL ARMSTRONG'S WALK ON THE MOON; ARTIST: ELMER LEHNHARDT				
AL	1969	R: 6	EMBOSSED STANDARD BOX $100	MATCHING ROUND PLASTIC BOTTLE $60

14. bottle

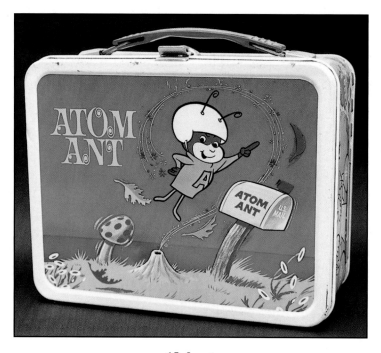

15. front

15. ATOM ANT				
BASED ON THE HANNA-BARBERA CARTOON TV SERIES; ARTIST: NICK LoBIANCO				
KST	1966	R: 6	STANDARD BOX $150	MATCHING STEEL/GLASS BOTTLE $80

15. back

15. bottle

16. front

16. back

16. AUTO RACE (w/SPIN GAME)					
ARTIST: NICK LoBIANCO					
KST	1967	R: 5	STANDARD BOX $95	MATCHING STEEL/GLASS BOTTLE $45
			STANDARD BOX w/GAME PIECES $190	

16. bottle

17. bottle

17. BACK IN '76					
ARTIST: ELMER LEHNHARDT					
AL	1975	R: 5	STANDARD BOX $75	MATCHING ROUND PLASTIC BOTTLE $35

18. front & bottle

18. back

		18. BATMAN		
		BASED ON THE TV SERIES; ARTIST: ELMER LEHNHARDT		
AL	1966 – 1967	R: 6	EMBOSSED STANDARD BOX $200	MATCHING STEEL/GLASS BOTTLE $110

19. front

19. back

19. bottle

		19. BATTLE KIT		
		ARTISTS: NICK LoBIANCO & T. OUGHTEN		
KST	1965 – 1966	R: 5	STANDARD BOX $95	MATCHING STEEL/GLASS BOTTLE $60

20. front

20. back

20. BATTLE OF THE PLANETS				
BASED ON THE TV SERIES				
KST	1979	R: 4	STANDARD BOX $55	MATCHING SQUARE PLASTIC BOTTLE $30

21. front

21. back

21. BATTLESTAR GALACTICA				
BASED ON THE TV SERIES; ARTIST: ELMER LEHNHARDT				
AL	1978	R: 3	EMBOSSED STANDARD BOX $50	MATCHING ROUND PLASTIC BOTTLE $25

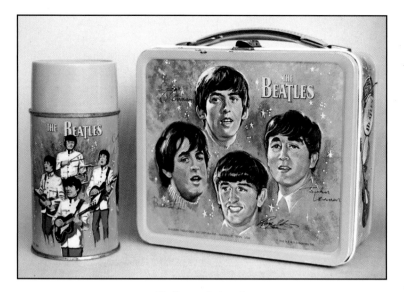

22. front & bottle

22. back

22. THE BEATLES				
ARTIST: ELMER LEHNHARDT (FROM PHOTOS BY D. HOFFMAN)				
VERY POPULAR! A CONDITION 10 KIT (BOX AND BOTTLE) WOULD BE AS HIGH AS $1,500 – 2,000.				
AL	1966 – 1967	R: 8	STANDARD BOX $750	MATCHING STEEL/GLASS BOTTLE $425

23. front

23. back

23. bottle

23. BEDKNOBS and BROOMSTICKS				
BASED ON THE DISNEY MOVIE; ARTIST: ELMER LEHNHARDT				
AL	1972	R: 4	EMBOSSED STANDARD BOX $70	MATCHING ROUND PLASTIC BOTTLE $50
				GENERIC PLASTIC BOTTLE $15

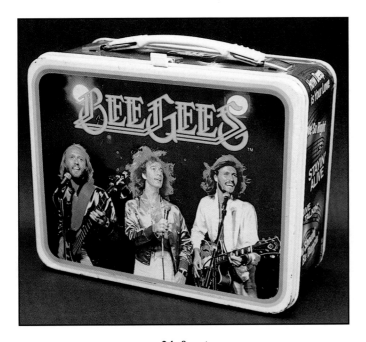

24. bottle

24. front

24. BEEGEES: BARRY, MAURICE & ROBIN				
THREE BOXES WERE MADE; ALL HAVE SAME FRONT, BUT EACH ONE HAS A DIFFERENT BEEGEE ON THE BACK.				
KST	1978	R: 4	STANDARD BOX $50	MATCHING SQUARE PLASTIC BOTTLE $30

25. front

25. back

25. BERENSTAIN BEARS				
BASED ON THE BOOKS; ARTISTS: STAN & JAN BERENSTAIN				
AT	1983	R: 4	STANDARD BOX $50	MATCHING SQUARE PLASTIC BOTTLE $25

26. front

26. back

26. BETSY CLARK (a.k.a. HALLMARK KIDS) BLUE				
KST	1976	R: 3	STANDARD BOX $40	MATCHING SQUARE PLASTIC BOTTLE $20

27. front

27. back

27. bottle

27. BETSY CLARK (a.k.a. HALLMARK KIDS) YELLOW				
KST	1976	R: 3	STANDARD BOX $40	MATCHING SQUARE PLASTIC BOTTLE $20

28. front & bottle

28. back

28. BEVERLY HILLBILLIES BASED ON THE TV SERIES				
AL	1963	R: 6	STANDARD BOX $175	MATCHING STEEL/GLASS BOTTLE $95

29. back

29. front

29. "BICYCLE RIDERS"				
COLLECTION SORFIM, ROUEN, FRANCE	1981	R: 9	BOX $125	BOTTLE UNKNOWN

30. front & bottle

30. back

30. BIONIC WOMAN (WITH CAR)				
BASED ON THE TV SERIES STARRING LINDSAY WAGNER; ARTIST: ELMER LEHNHARDT				
AL	1977	R: 4	EMBOSSED STANDARD BOX $75	MATCHING SQUARE PLASTIC BOTTLE $35

31. front

31. back

31. BIONIC WOMAN (WITH DOG)				
ARTIST: ELMER LEHNHARDT				
AL	1977	R: 4	EMBOSSED STANDARD BOX $75	USES SAME BOTTLE AS "BIONIC WOMAN WITH CAR" BOX

32. front

32. *THE BLACK HOLE*				
BASED ON THE DISNEY MOVIE				
AL	1979	R: 4	STANDARD BOX $75	MATCHING ROUND PLASTIC BOTTLE $40

32. back

32. bottle

33. front

33. BLONDIE				
MADE FOR THE TV SITCOM; ARTIST: NICK LoBIANCO				
KST	1969	R: 6	STANDARD BOX $150	MATCHING SQUARE PLASTIC BOTTLE $85

33. back

33. bottle

34. front & bottle

34. back

34. BOATING				
ARTIST: ED WEXLER				
AT	1959 – 1961	R: 8	STANDARD BOX $385	MATCHING STEEL/GLASS BOTTLE $150

35. bottle

35. BOBBY SHERMAN				
DESIGNED BY ARTIST NICK LoBIANCO FROM FAN MAGAZINE PICTURES				
KST	1972	R: 5	STANDARD BOX $100	MATCHING STEEL/GLASS BOTTLE $60

36. front

36. BONANZA (GREEN) ARTIST: ELMER LEHNHARDT				
AL	1963	R: 6	STANDARD BOX $150	MATCHING STEEL/GLASS BOTTLE $80

36. back

36. bottle

37. front

37. back

37. BONANZA (BROWN) ARTIST: ELMER LEHNHARDT				
AL	1965	R: 5	STANDARD BOX $135	MATCHING STEEL/GLASS BOTTLE $75

38. front

38. BOND XX SECRET AGENT ARTIST: JESS HAGER				
OA	1966 – 1967	R: 7	STANDARD BOX $250	NO MATCHING BOTTLE MADE

39. front

	39. BOZO THE CLOWN BASED ON THE TV SERIES: ARTIST: ELMER LEHNHARDT			
AL	1963	R: 7	DOME BOX $300	MATCHING STEEL/GLASS BOTTLE $150

39. back

39. bottle

40. front

41. bottle

40. THE BRADY BUNCH
BASED ON THE TV SERIES STARRING FLORENCE HENDERSON; ARTIST: NICK LoBIANCO

KST	1970	R: 6	STANDARD BOX $250	MATCHING STEEL/GLASS BOTTLE $125

41. BRAVE EAGLE
(BOX CAME WITH BLUE, GREEN OR RED BAND) ARTIST: ED WEXLER

AT	1957	R: 7	STANDARD BOX $225	STEEL/GLASS BOTTLE $115

42. BREAD DOME BOX (POP ART BREAD DOME BOX)
ATTRIBUTED TO ARTIST: ELMER LEHNHARDT

AL	1968	R: 7	DOME BOX $300	MATCHING ROUND PLASTIC CAMPBELL SOUP BOTTLE $140

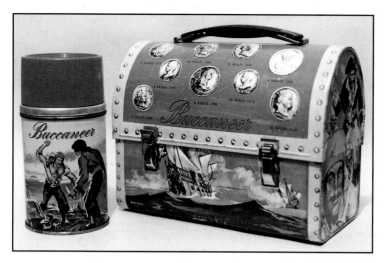

43. front & bottle

43. back

43. BUCCANEER DOME BOX				
ARTIST: BOB BURTON, WHOSE SELF-PORTRAIT APPEARS ON THE "10 REALES" COIN				
AL	1957	R: 7	DOME BOX $250	MATCHING STEEL/GLASS BOTTLE $150

44. front

44. back

44. bottle

44. BUCK ROGERS IN THE 25TH CENTURY				
BASED ON THE TV SERIES; ARTISTS: BEVERLY BURGE & JOHN HENRY				
AL	1980 – 1982	R: 3	EMBOSSED STANDARD BOX $50	MATCHING ROUND PLASTIC BOTTLE $25

45. bottle

46. front

			45. BUGALOOS	
			BASED ON THE TV SERIES; ARTIST: ELMER LEHNHARDT	
AL	1971	R: 4	STANDARD BOX $125	MATCHING ROUND PLASTIC BOTTLE $45

			46. BULLWINKLE & ROCKY	
			BASED ON THE TV CARTOON SERIES	
UN	1962	R: 9	STANDARD BOX $1,000	MATCHING STEEL/GLASS BOTTLE $750

47. front & bottle

			47. CABBAGE PATCH KIDS	
			ARTIST: LEO SCHIEN; SAME FRONT & BACK	
KST	1984	R: 2	STANDARD BOX $25	MATCHING SQUARE PLASTIC BOTTLE $10

43

48. front & bottle

48. CABLE CAR DOME BOX (ALADDIN CABLE CAR)				
ARTISTS: BOB BURTON & ELMER LEHNHARDT				
AL	1962	R: 8	DOME BOX $425	MATCHING STEEL/GLASS BOTTLE $200

48. back

49. front

49. CAMPUS QUEEN (w/MAGNETIC GAME ON BACK)					
ARTIST: NICK LoBIANCO					
KST	1967	R: 4	STANDARD BOX w/GAME $190	MATCHING STEEL/GLASS BOTTLE $35	
			STANDARD BOX w/o GAME $75		

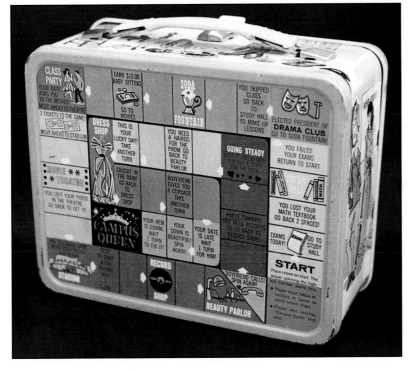

49. back

49. bottle

50. front   **50. back**

50. CANADIAN PACIFIC TRAIN				
OA	1970	R: 4	STANDARD BOX $90	NO MATCHING BOTTLE MADE

51. front

51. CAPTAIN ASTRO				
A SPACE TOY CHARACTER; ART BY JESS HAGER; SAME FRONT & BACK				
OA	1970	R: 7	STANDARD BOX $350	NO MATCHING BOTTLE MADE

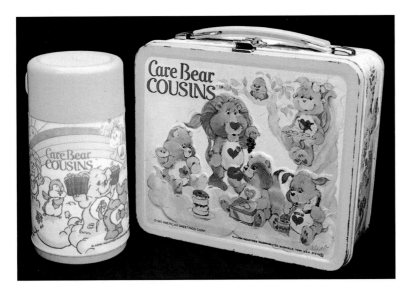

52. front & bottle

52. back

		52. CARE BEAR COUSINS BASED ON THE TV SERIES & TOYS		
AL	1985 – 1986	R: 2	EMBOSSED STANDARD BOX $30	MATCHING ROUND PLASTIC BOTTLE $10

53. front

53. back

		53. CARE BEARS		
AL	1984 – 1985	R: 2	EMBOSSED STANDARD BOX $30	MATCHING ROUND PLASTIC BOTTLE $10

47

54. front

54. bottle

54. CARNIVAL SAME FRONT & BACK				
UN	1959	R: 8	STANDARD BOX $650	MATCHING STEEL/GLASS BOTTLE $275

55. front & bottle

55. back

55. CARTOON ZOO BASED ON THE HANNA-BARBERA TV CARTOON SERIES				
UN	1962 – 1963	R: 7	STANDARD BOX $500	MATCHING STEEL/GLASS BOTTLE $200

56. bottle

57. front

56. CASEY JONES				
(CAB INSCRIBED "L.F. & C.R.R." FOR LANDERS, FRARY & CLARK)				
UN	1960	R: 9	DOME BOX $600	MATCHING STEEL/GLASS BOTTLE $200

57. THE CHAN CLAN				
BASED ON THE HANNA-BARBERA TV SERIES; ARTIST: NICK LoBIANCO				
KST	1973	R: 6	STANDARD BOX $125	MATCHING SQUARE PLASTIC BOTTLE $45

57. bottle

57. back

58. front & bottle

58. back

58. CHARLIE'S ANGELS				
BASED ON THE TV SERIES AFTER FARAH FAWCETT HAD LEFT, FEATURING KATE JACKSON, CHERYL LADD & JACLYN SMITH; ARTIST: ELMER LEHNHARDT				
AL	1978 – 1979	R: 4	EMBOSSED STANDARD BOX $75	MATCHING ROUND PLASTIC BOTTLE $35

59. front

60. bottle

59. CHILDREN (a.k.a. ART NOUVEAU CHILDREN)				
UNK	1920s	R: 8	CARRY-ALL BOX $115	NO BOTTLE MADE

60. CHITTY CHITTY BANG BANG				
BASED ON THE DISNEY MOVIE				
KST	1969	R: 6	STANDARD BOX $125	MATCHING STEEL/GLASS BOTTLE $60

61. front & bottle

61. back

61. CHUCK WAGON ARTIST: BOB BURTON				
AL	1958	R: 7	DOME BOX $250	MATCHING STEEL/GLASS BOTTLE $100

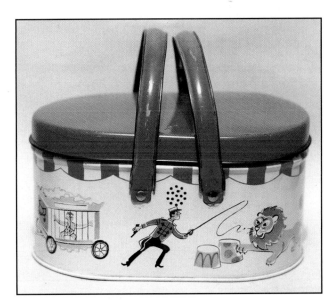

62. front

62. back

62. CIRCUS				
UNK	1930s – 1940s	R: 7	CARRY-ALL BOX $125	NO BOTTLE MADE

63. front & bottle

63. back

63. CIRCUS WAGON				
AT	1958	R: 8	DOME BOX $370	MATCHING STEEL/GLASS BOTTLE $135

64. front

64. back

64. CLASH OF THE TITANS				
BASED ON THE MOVIE STARRING HARRY HAMLIN; ARTIST: DON HENRY				
KST	1981	R: 5	STANDARD BOX $75	MATCHING SQUARE PLASTIC BOTTLE $35

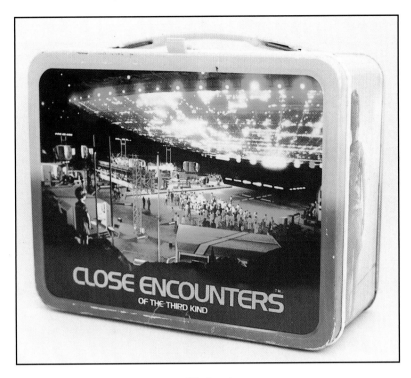

65. front

			65. CLOSE ENCOUNTERS BASED ON THE MOVIE	
KST	1981	R: 4	STANDARD BOX $70	YELLOW MATCHING SQUARE PLASTIC BOTTLE $50
				RED MATCHING SQUARE PLASTIC BOTTLE w/WHITE CUP $45

65. back

65. bottle

66. front

66. back

66. COL. ED McCAULEY				
BASED ON THE SHORT-LIVED TV SERIES *MEN INTO SPACE*; ARTIST: ELMER LEHNHARDT				
AL	1960	R: 7	STANDARD BOX $300	MATCHING STEEL/GLASS BOTTLE $140

66. bottle

67. bottle

67. CORSAGE (BLUE)				
BLUE WAS THE FIRST COLOR; THE BLUE BOX IS IDENTICAL TO THE PINK 1964 ONE EXCEPT FOR THE COLOR				
AT	1958	R: 5	STANDARD BOX $70	MATCHING STEEL/GLASS BOTTLE $45

68. front & bottle

68. CORSAGE (PINK)				
SAME FRONT & BACK				
AT	1964	R: 5	STANDARD BOX $70	MATCHING STEEL/GLASS BOTTLE $45

69. front

69. bottle

69. CORSAGE (LIGHT BLUE)				
SAME FRONT & BACK				
KST	1963 – 1964	R: 5	STANDARD BOX $70	MATCHING STEEL/GLASS BOTTLE $45

70. bottle

71. front

70. CORSAGE (LIGHT BLUE)				
SAME BOX AS THE 1963 – 1964 CORSAGE BUT HAS THERMOS LOGO ON THE FRONT & CAME WITH SHORT BOTTLE				
AT	1964 – 1972	R: 5	STANDARD BOX $70	MATCHING STEEL/GLASS BOTTLE $45

71. back

71. bottle

71. COWBOY IN AFRICA				
BASED ON THE TV SERIES; ARTIST: NICK LoBIANCO				
KST	1968	R: 6	STANDARD BOX $210	MATCHING STEEL/GLASS BOTTLE $100

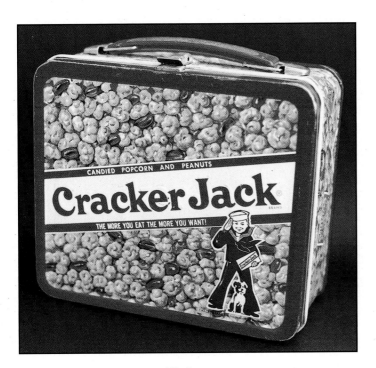

72. bottle

72. front

72. CRACKER JACK			
ARTIST: ELMER LEHNHARDT; SAME FRONT & BACK			
AL	1979	R: 5	EMBOSSED STANDARD BOX $80	MATCHING ROUND PLASTIC BOTTLE $40

73.

73. CRACKER JACK			
SAME FRONT & BACK			
CHEINCO	1979	R: 4	CARRY-ALL BOX $50	NO BOTTLE MADE

74. front & bottle

74. back

74. CURIOSITY SHOP				
BASED ON THE TV SERIES; ARTIST: NICK LoBIANCO				
KST	1972	R: 5	STANDARD BOX $80	MATCHING STEEL/GLASS BOTTLE $45

75. front

75. back

75. bottle

75. THE DARK CRYSTAL				
BASED ON THE MOVIE				
KST	1982	R: 3	STANDARD BOX $35	MATCHING SQUARE PLASTIC BOTTLE $20

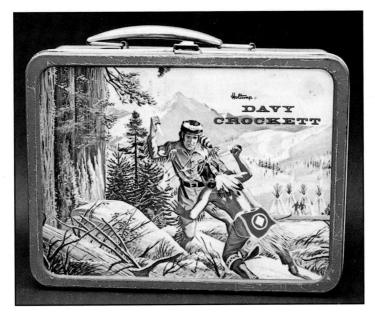

76. front

76. DAVY CROCKETT (GREEN RIM)				
BASED ON THE TV SERIES; DISNEY FORCED AMERICAN THERMOS TO CEASE PRODUCTION OF THIS UNLICENSED KIT; ARTIST: ED WEXLER				
AT	1955	R:7	STANDARD BOX $175	MATCHING STEEL/GLASS BOTTLE $110

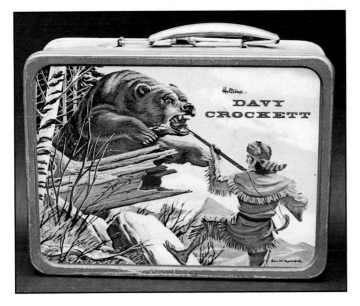

76. back

76. bottle

77. front

77. back

77. DAVY CROCKETT (OFFICIAL)				
K	1955	R: 8	STANDARD BOX $285	NO MATCHING BOTTLE MADE

78. front

78. DAVY CROCKETT/INDIAN				
AD	1955	R: 8	STANDARD BOX $285	MATCHING STEEL/GLASS BOTTLE $2,000

79. front

79. back

79. DAVY CROCKETT & KIT CARSON				
THE BOX THAT LOST ADCO THEIR DISNEY LICENSE BECAUSE THEY INCLUDED KIT CARSON, AN UNLICENSED, NON-DISNEY CHARACTER				
AD	1955	R: 8	STANDARD BOX $265 (BANDS MADE WITH THREE DIFFERENT SCENES)	NO MATCHING BOTTLE MADE

80. front & bottle

80. DEBUTANTE				
DESIGNER: BOB BURTON; SAME FRONT & BACK				
AL	1958	R: 7	MAKE-UP KIT OR PURSE-STYLE BOX $150	MATCHING STEEL/GLASS BOTTLE $75

81. front & bottle

81. back

			81. DENIM DINER	
AL	1975	R: 5	DOME BOX $110	MATCHING ROUND PLASTIC BOTTLE $30

82. front

82. back

82. bottle

			82. DICK TRACY	
			BASED ON THE COMIC STRIP CHARACTER	
AL	1967	R: 6	EMBOSSED STANDARD BOX $175	STEEL/GLASS BOTTLE $100

83. front

			83. *DISCO* ARTIST: BOB JONES	
AL	1979 – 1980	R: 4	STANDARD BOX $60	MATCHING ROUND PLASTIC BOTTLE $25

83. back

83. bottle

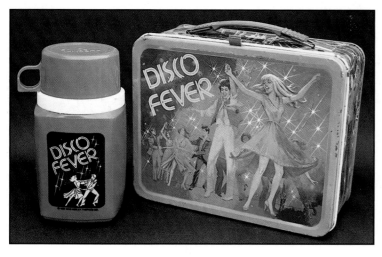

84. front & bottle

84. back

84. DISCO FEVER ARTIST: GENE LEMERY				
AL	1980	R: 4	STANDARD BOX $60	MATCHING SQUARE PLASTIC BOTTLE $30

85. front

85. back

85. DISNEY EXPRESS! ARTIST: BEVERLY BURGE				
AL	1979 – 1980	R: 2	EMBOSSED STANDARD BOX $30	MATCHING ROUND PLASTIC BOTTLE $75

86. front & bottle

86. back

86. DISNEY FIREFIGHTERS				
AL	1980	R: 6	DOME BOX $175	MATCHING ROUND PLASTIC BOTTLE $75

87. front & bottle

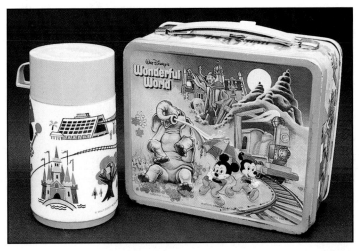

87. back & bottle

87. DISNEY MAGIC KINGDOM/WONDERFUL WORLD ARTIST: BOB JONES				
AL	1980 – 1982	R: 2	EMBOSSED STANDARD BOX $25	MATCHING ROUND PLASTIC BOTTLE $15

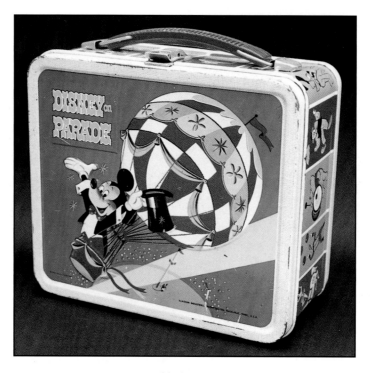

88. front

		88. DISNEY ON PARADE BASED ON THE DISNEY ROAD SHOWS		
AL	1970 – 1971	R: 4	EMBOSSED STANDARD BOX $35	MATCHING ROUND PLASTIC BOTTLE $30

88. back

88. bottle

89. front

89. bottle

89. DISNEY SCHOOL BUS				
THE LONGEST-RUNNING AND MOST PROLIFIC BOX IN HISTORY CAME IN BOTH ORANGE AND YELLOW; IDEA: AL KONETZNI; ARTIST: ELMER LEHNHARDT				
AL	1961 – 1973	R: 5	DOME BOX $120	1961 – 1967 MATCHING STEEL/GLASS BOTTLE $55
				1968 – 1973 MATCHING ROUND PLASTIC BOTTLE $40

89. back

89. bottle

90. front

90. back

90. WALT DISNEY'S WONDERFUL WORLD/WORLD ON ICE				
AL	1982	R: 2	STANDARD BOX $25	MATCHING ROUND PLASTIC BOTTLE $15

90. bottle

91. front

91. back

91. WALT DISNEY WORLD (BLUE RIM)				
AL	1970	R:2	EMBOSSED STANDARD BOX $35	MATCHING ROUND PLASTIC BOTTLE $20

92. front

92. back

92. DOCTOR DOLITTLE				
BASED ON THE MOVIE STARRING REX HARRISON; ARTIST: ELMER LEHNHARDT				
AL	1968	R: 5	EMBOSSED STANDARD BOX $105	MATCHING STEEL/GLASS BOTTLE $60

92. bottle

93. front

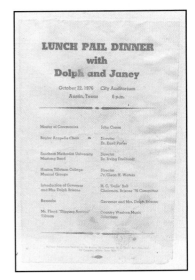

93. (invitation)

93. DOLPH BRISCOE				
WITH INVITATION TO DINNER WITH DOLPH AND JANEY ON OCTOBER 22, 1976				
AT	1970s	R: 9	DOME BOX w/INVITATION $150 BOX ALONE $100	NO BOTTLE KNOWN

94. front

94. back

94. bottle

94. THE DOUBLE DECKERS				
AL	1970	R: 5	STANDARD BOX $85	MATCHING ROUND PLASTIC BOTTLE $50

95. front

95. back

95. bottle

95. DRAG STRIP				
AL	1975 – 1977	R: 5	EMBOSSED OR FLAT STANDARD BOX $75	MATCHING ROUND PLASTIC BOTTLE $40

96. front

96. DRAGON'S LAIR				
AL	1983	R: 3	STANDARD BOX $45	MATCHING ROUND PLASTIC BOTTLE $25

96. back

96. bottle

97. bottle

98. front & bottle

97. *THE DUCHESS*				
AL	1960 – 1962	R: 7	STANDARD BOX $125	MATCHING STEEL/GLASS BOTTLE $60

98. *DUDLEY DO-RIGHT* BASED ON THE TV CARTOON SERIES; SAME FRONT & BACK				
UN	1962	BOX, R: 9 BOTTLE, R: 10	STANDARD BOX $2,000	MATCHING STEEL/GLASS BOTTLE $1,500

99. front & bottle

99. back

99. *THE DUKES OF HAZZARD (BOSS HOGG)* ARTIST: ELMER LEHNHARDT				
AL	1980	R: 5	EMBOSSED STANDARD BOX $70	MATCHING ROUND PLASTIC BOTTLE $25

100. front

100. back

100. THE DUKES OF HAZZARD (CAR) BASED ON THE TV SERIES; ARTIST: ELMER LEHNHARDT				
AL	1983	R: 4	EMBOSSED STANDARD BOX $65	USES SAME DUKES BOTTLE AS PREVIOUS BOX

101. front & bottle

101. DUTCH COTTAGE				
AT	1958	R: 9	DOME BOX $600	MATCHING STEEL/GLASS BOTTLE $250

102. front

			102. DYNOMUTT BASED ON THE HANNA-BARBERA TV CARTOON SERIES; ARTIST: NICK LoBIANCO	
KST	1977	R: 5	STANDARD BOX $75	MATCHING SQUARE PLASTIC BOTTLE $35

102. back

102. bottle

103. front

103. E.T.				
BASED ON THE MOVIE; ARTIST: ELMER LEHNHARDT				
AL	1982	R: 3	EMBOSSED STANDARD BOX $50	MATCHING ROUND PLASTIC BOTTLE w/SAD FACES (AS PICTURED) $30
				BOTTLE w/HAPPY FACES $30

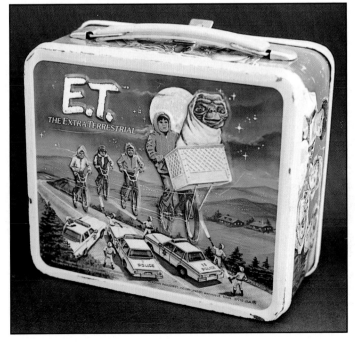

103. back

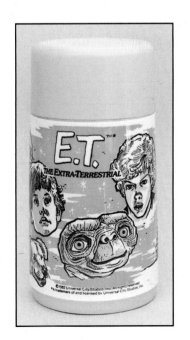

103. bottle

104. front

104. EARLY WEST (INDIAN TERRITORY)				
ARTIST: WILLIAM KULMAN				
OA	1982 – 1984	R: 5	STANDARD BOX $120	NO MATCHING BOTTLE MADE

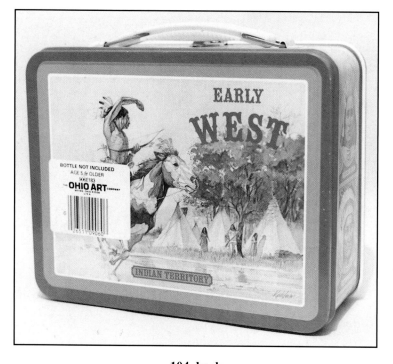

104. back

104. band

105. front

		105. EARLY WEST (OREGON TRAIL) ARTIST: WILLIAM KULMAN		
OA	1982 – 1984	R: 5	STANDARD BOX $120	NO MATCHING BOTTLE MADE

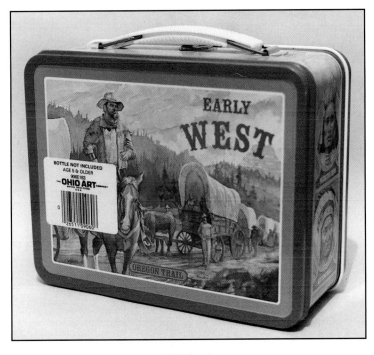

105. back

105. band

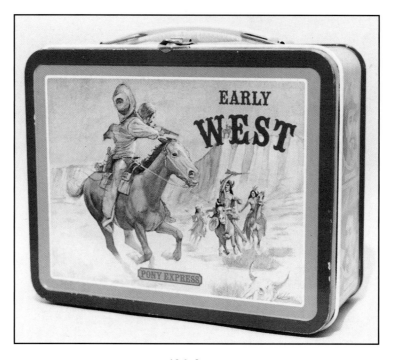

106. front

		106. EARLY WEST (PONY EXPRESS) ARTIST: WILLIAM KULMAN		
OA	1982 – 1984	R: 5	STANDARD BOX $120	NO MATCHING BOTTLE MADE

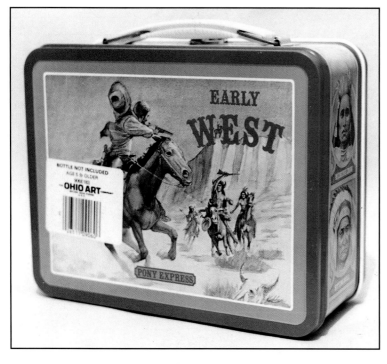

106. back

106. band

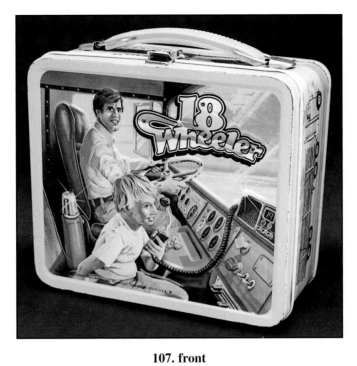

107. front

		107. 18 WHEELER ARTIST: BOB JONES		
AL	1978	R: 4	STANDARD BOX $65	MATCHING ROUND PLASTIC BOTTLE $30

107. back

107. bottle

108. front

108. back

109. bottle

108. EL CHAPULIN COLORADO				
MADE FOR EXPORT TO MEXICO, FEATURING A MEXICAN SITCOM; ARTIST: ELMER LEHNHARDT				
AL	1979	R: 4	EMBOSSED STANDARD BOX $70	MATCHING ROUND PLASTIC BOTTLE $40

109. front

109. back

109. EMERGENCY!				
STANDARD BOX & DOME BOX BOTH BASED ON THE TV SERIES				
AL	1973	R: 4	STANDARD BOX $75	MATCHING ROUND PLASTIC BOTTLE $40

110. front

110. back

110. EMERGENCY!				
AL	1977	R: 7	DOME BOX $200	SAME BOTTLE AS STANDARD BOX

111. front

111. back

111. bottle

111. THE EMPIRE STRIKES BACK (SHIP) BASED ON THE MOVIE; ARTIST: DON HENRY				
KST	1980	R: 3	STANDARD BOX $45	MATCHING SQUARE PLASTIC BOTTLE $20

112. front

<div align="center">***112. THE EMPIRE STRIKES BACK (SWAMP)*** ARTIST: GENE LEMERY</div>				
KST	1981	R: 3	STANDARD BOX $45	MATCHING SQUARE PLASTIC BOTTLE $20 (ORIGINALLY CAME WITH YELLOW CUP)

112. back

112. bottle

113. front

113. EVEL KNIEVEL			
ONE OF AMERICA'S DAREDEVILS; BACK OF BOX FEATURES FAILED ATTEMPT TO JUMP THE SNAKE RIVER ARTIST: JOHN HENRY			
AL	1974	R: 4	EMBOSSED STANDARD BOX $100	MATCHING ROUND PLASTIC BOTTLE $50

113. bottle

113. back

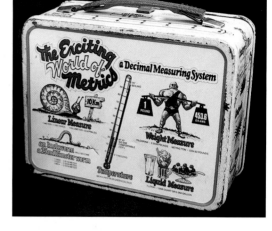

114. front & bottle

114. back

114. THE EXCITING WORLD OF METRICS ARTIST: DON HENRY				
KST	1976 – 77	R: 4	STANDARD BOX $65	MATCHING SQUARE PLASTIC BOTTLE $35

115. front

115. back

115. bottle

115. THE FALL GUY BASED ON THE TV SERIES STARRING LEE MAJORS; ARTIST: ELMER LEHNHARDT				
AL	1982 – 1983	R: 5	EMBOSSED STANDARD BOX $75	MATCHING ROUND PLASTIC BOTTLE $35

116. bottle

117. bottle

116. FAMILY AFFAIR BASED ON THE TV SERIES; ARTIST: NICK LoBIANCO				
KST	1969 – 1970	R: 5	STANDARD BOX $80	MATCHING STEEL/GLASS BOTTLE $45

117. FESS PARKER/DANIEL BOONE SHOW ARTISTS: NICK LoBIANCO & T. OUGHTEN				
KST	1965 – 1966	R: 7	STANDARD BOX $190	MATCHING STEEL/GLASS BOTTLE $120

117. front

117. back

118. front

118. bottle

118. FIREBALL XL5					
			ARTIST: WALLY WOOD		
KST	1964 – 1965	R: 6	STANDARD BOX $250	MATCHING STEEL/GLASS BOTTLE $85	
				BOTTLE MADE 1" SHORTER THE SECOND YEAR	

118. back

119. front & bottle

		119. FIREHOUSE/CENTRAL STATION ART ATTRIBUTED TO ED WEXLER		
AT	1959 – 1960	R: 8	DOME BOX $380	MATCHING STEEL/GLASS BOTTLE $160

119. back

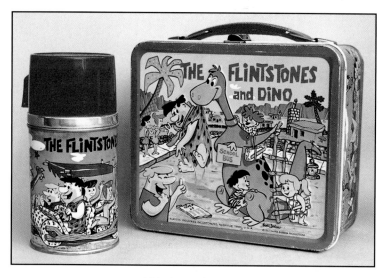

120. front & bottle

120. back

			120. THE FLINTSTONES (AND DINO)	
			CHARACTERS FROM THE HANNA-BARBERA TV CARTOON SERIES; ARTIST: ELMER LEHNHARDT	
AL	1962	R: 6	EMBOSSED STANDARD BOX $250	MATCHING STEEL/GLASS BOTTLE $100

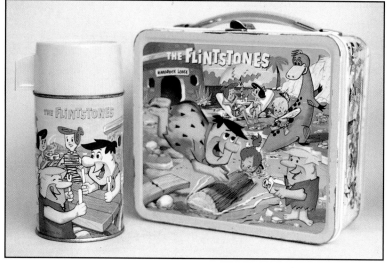

121. front & bottle

121. back

			121. THE FLINTSTONES (YELLOW RIM)	
AL	1964	R: 6	STANDARD BOX $200	MATCHING STEEL/GLASS BOTTLE $110

122. front

122. THE FLINTSTONES				
AL	1971	R: 5	STANDARD BOX $135	MATCHING PLASTIC BOTTLE $75

122. bottle

122. back

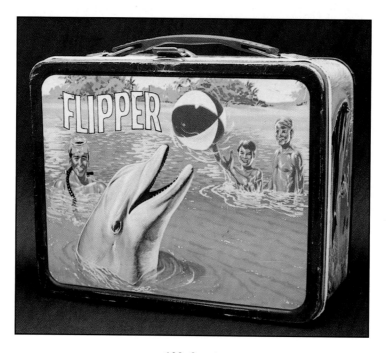

123. front

123. FLIPPER				
BASED ON THE TV SERIES; ARTIST: NICK LoBIANCO				
KST	1966	R: 6	STANDARD BOX $150	MATCHING STEEL/GLASS BOTTLE $75

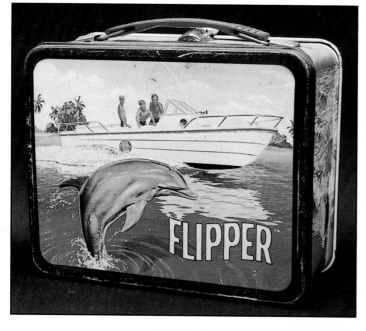

123. back

123. bottle

124. front

124. FLORAL SAME FRONT & BACK				
OA	1970 – 1971	R: 3	STANDARD BOX $50	NO MATCHING BOTTLE MADE

125. front

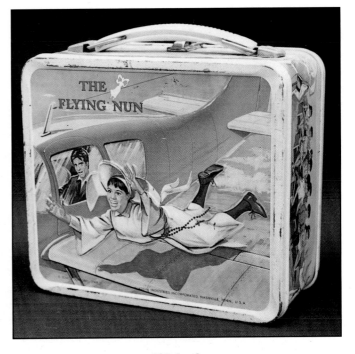

125. back

125. FLYING NUN BASED ON THE TV SERIES STARRING SALLY FIELD; ARTIST: ELMER LEHNHARDT				
AL	1968	R: 6	STANDARD BOX $175	MATCHING STEEL/GLASS BOTTLE $80

126. front

126. THE FOX AND THE HOUND				
BASED ON THE DISNEY MOVIE; ARTIST: BEVERLY BURGE				
AL	1981	R: 3	EMBOSSED STANDARD BOX $45	MATCHING ROUND PLASTIC BOTTLE $20

126. back

126. bottle

127. front

127. FRAGGLE ROCK				
BASED ON THE TV SERIES; ARTIST: GENE LEMERY				
KST	1984	R: 3	STANDARD BOX $45	MATCHING SQUARE PLASTIC BOTTLE $20

127. back

127. bottle

128. front

128. FRITOS				
(PREMIUM GIVEN TO HIGH VOLUME LUNCHBOX RETAILERS BY KST)				
KST	1975	R: 6	STANDARD BOX $125	NO MATCHING BOTTLE MADE

129. front

129. back

129. FRUIT BASKET (GREEN BACKGROUND)				
ALSO MADE WITH BROWN BACKGROUND				
OA	1975 – 1976	R: 4	STANDARD BOX/ GREEN $35	NO MATCHING BOTTLE MADE
			STANDARD BOX/BROWN $35	

130. front

130. back

130. FUNTASTIC WORLD OF HANNA-BARBERA				
KST	1978	R: 4	STANDARD BOX $75	MATCHING SQUARE PLASTIC BOTTLE $35

131. G.I. JOE BASED ON THE ACTION FIGURES; FRONT OF BOX IS BATTLE SCENE; BACK IS SCUBA DIVERS; ARTIST: NICK LoBIANCO				
KST	1967 – 1968	R: 6	STANDARD BOX $150	MATCHING STEEL/GLASS BOTTLE $85

131. bottle

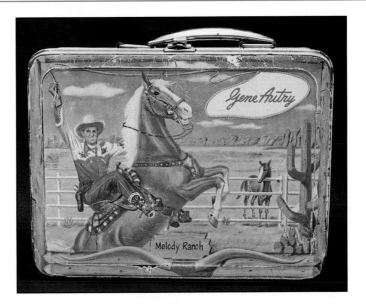

132. front

132. bottle

132. GENE AUTRY BACK & BANDS ARE HORSEHIDE PATTERN				
UN	1954 – 1955	R: 8	STANDARD BOX $500	MATCHING STEEL/GLASS BOTTLE $350

133. front

133. bottle

133. GENTLE BEN				
BASED ON THE TV SERIES; ARTIST: ELMER LEHNHARDT				
AL	1968	R: 6	EMBOSSED STANDARD BOX $115	MATCHING STEEL/GLASS BOTTLE $80
				MATCHING ROUND PLASTIC BOTTLE $50

133. back

133. bottle

134. front

134. GET SMART				
BASED ON THE TV SERIES; ARTIST: NICK LoBIANCO				
KST	1966	R: 7	STANDARD BOX $200	MATCHING STEEL/GLASS BOTTLE $100

135. back

135. front

135. GIRL SCOUTS				
NYM	1920s – 1930s	R: 8	CARRY-ALL BOX $95	NO BOTTLE MADE

136. front & bottle

		136. GLOBE-TROTTER ARTIST: BOB BURTON		
AL	1959	R: 7	DOME BOX $270	MATCHING STEEL/GLASS BOTTLE $125

136. back

137. bottle

		137. GOMER PYLE BASED ON THE TV SERIES; ARTIST: ELMER LEHNHARDT		
AL	1966	R: 6	EMBOSSED STANDARD BOX $200	MATCHING STEEL/GLASS BOTTLE $110

138. front

140. bottle

138. GOOD LUCK BINGO				
CHEINCO	1980s	R: 5	CARRY-ALL BOX $65	NO BOTTLE MADE

139. GOOBER AND THE GHOST CHASERS/INCH HIGH PRIVATE EYE BASED ON THE HANNA-BARBERA TV CARTOON SERIES; ARTIST: NICK LoBIANCO				
KST	1974	R: 4	STANDARD BOX $60	MATCHING SQUARE PLASTIC BOTTLE $25

139. front

139. back

140. GREAT WILD WEST				
UN	1959 – 1969	R: 8	STANDARD BOX $460	MATCHING STEEL/GLASS BOTTLE $210

141. front

141. GREEN AND GRAY				
AT	1950s	R: 5	STANDARD BOX $30	GENERIC STEEL/GLASS BOTTLE $25

142. front & bottle

142. back

142. THE GREEN HORNET BASED ON THE TV SERIES; ARTIST: NICK LoBIANCO				
KST	1967	R: 8	STANDARD BOX $500	MATCHING STEEL/GLASS BOTTLE $250

143. front

143. GREMLINS				
BASED ON THE MOVIE				
AL	1984	R: 2	STANDARD BOX $35	MATCHING ROUND PLASTIC BOTTLE $15

143. back

143. bottle

144. front & bottle

144. GRIZZLY ADAMS				
BASED ON THE TV SERIES; THE LAST OF THE OLDER DOMES MADE				
AL	1977	R: 6	DOME BOX $150	MATCHING ROUND PLASTIC BOTTLE $50

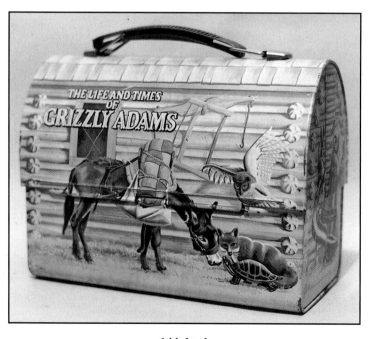

144. back

145. bottle

145. THE GUNS OF WILL SONNETT				
BASED ON THE TV SERIES; ARTIST: NICK LoBIANCO				
KST	1968	R: 6	STANDARD BOX $180	MATCHING STEEL/GLASS BOTTLE $100

146. bottle

147. bottle

146. GUNSMOKE				
ARTIST: ELMER LEHNHARDT; FRONT OF BOX IS MATT ON HORSEBACK WITH GUN POINTING DOWN AT ROBBERS				
AL	1962	R: 7	STANDARD BOX $210	MATCHING STEEL/GLASS BOTTLE $95

147. front

147. back

147. GUNSMOKE				
AL	1973	R: 6	STANDARD BOX $165	MATCHING ROUND PLASTIC BOTTLE $65

148. front

148. H.R. PUFNSTUF
CHARACTERS FROM THE KROFFT TV CARTOON SERIES; ARTIST: ELMER LEHNHARDT

AL	1970	R: 6	EMBOSSED STANDARD BOX $200	MATCHING ROUND PLASTIC BOTTLE $100

148. back

148. bottle

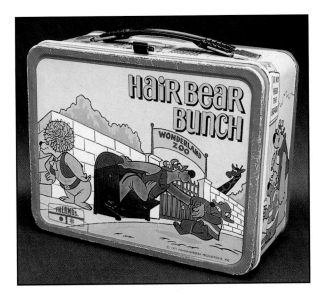

149. front

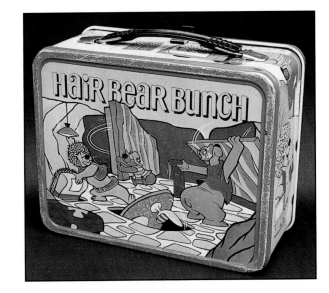

149. back

149. HAIR BEAR BUNCH				
BASED ON THE HANNA-BARBERA TV SERIES; ARTIST: NICK LoBIANCO				
KST	1972 – 1973	R: 4	STANDARD BOX $70	MATCHING SQUARE PLASTIC BOTTLE $35

150. front

150. back

150. HANSEL AND GRETEL				
WITH ORIGINAL K-MART $3.88 PRICE STICKER ON BACK				
OA	1982 – 1984	R: 5	STANDARD BOX $100	NO MATCHING BOTTLE MADE

151. front

151. HAPPY DAYS				
BASED ON THE TV SERIES; ARTIST: GENE LEMERY				
KST	1977	R: 4	STANDARD BOX $60	MATCHING SQUARE PLASTIC BOTTLE $30

151. back

151. bottle

152. front

152. back

152. HAPPY DAYS "THE FONZ"				
CAPITALIZING ON THE TV SHOW'S MOST POPULAR CHARACTER; ARTIST: GENE LEMERY				
KST	1978	R: 4	STANDARD BOX $60	MATCHING SQUARE PLASTIC BOTTLE (YELLOW) $30

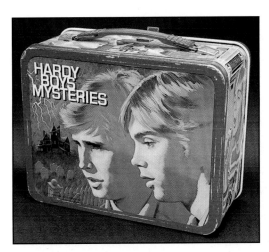

153. front

153. back

153. bottle

153. HARDY BOYS MYSTERIES				
BASED ON THE TV SERIES STARRING SHAUN CASSIDY & PARKER STEPHENSON; ARTIST: GENE LEMERY				
KST	1977	R: 4	STANDARD BOX $75	MATCHING SQUARE PLASTIC BOTTLE $30

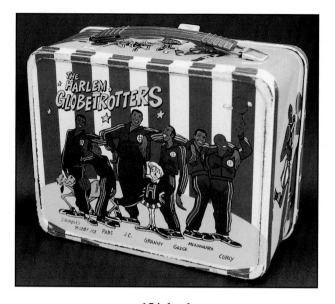

154. front

154. back

154. THE HARLEM GLOBETROTTERS
BASED ON THE HANNA-BARBERA CARTOON TV SERIES; MADE WITH EITHER BLUE UNIFORMS OR PURPLE UNIFORMS; ARTIST: NICK LOBIANCO

KST	1971	R: 5	STANDARD BOX (BLUE OR PURPLE) $75	MATCHING STEEL/GLASS BOTTLE $50

155. front & bottle

155. back

155. HE-MAN/MASTERS OF THE UNIVERSE
BASED ON THE TOYS AND THE TV SERIES

AL	1984	R: 2	STANDARD BOX $25	MATCHING ROUND PLASTIC BOTTLE $15

156. front & bottle

156. back

156. HEATHCLIFF				
BASED ON THE TV CARTOON SERIES; ARTIST: BRENDA BASLER				
AL	1982 – 1983	R: 3	EMBOSSED STANDARD BOX $35	MATCHING ROUND PLASTIC BOTTLE $15

157. front & bottle

157. back

157. HECTOR HEATHCOTE				
BASED ON THE TV CARTOON SERIES				
AL	1964	R: 7	STANDARD BOX $300	MATCHING STEEL/GLASS BOTTLE $150

158. bottle

159. front

			158. HEE HAW	
			BASED ON THE TV SERIES; ARTIST: NICK LoBIANCO	
KST	1971	R: 5	STANDARD BOX $100	MATCHING STEEL/GLASS BOTTLE $55

			159. HIGHWAY SIGNS (FIRST VERSION)	
			SAME FRONT & BACK	
OA	1968	R: 5	STANDARD BOX $80	NO MATCHING BOTTLE MADE

160. front

			160. HIGHWAY SIGNS (SECOND VERSION)	
			SAME FRONT & BACK	
OA	1972	R: 5	STANDARD BOX $80	NO MATCHING BOTTLE MADE

161. back

161. front & bottle

161. HOGAN'S HEROES BASED ON THE TV SERIES; ARTIST: ELMER LEHNHARDT				
AL	1966	R: 8	DOME BOX $400	MATCHING STEEL/GLASS BOTTLE $200

162. front

162. back

162. bottle

162. HOLLY HOBBIE (PARK BENCH/FALL SCENE) ARTIST: ANN CUMMINGS				
AL	1973 – 1974	R: 3	EMBOSSED STANDARD BOX $35	MATCHING ROUND PLASTIC BOTTLE $15 (ONE OF TWO FOR THIS BOX; THE SECOND ONE SHOWS A CAT ON A FENCE)

163. front

163. back

163. HOLLY HOBBIE (DARK BLUE RIM)				
ARTIST: ANN CUMMINGS				
AL	1975 – 1979	R: 2	EMBOSSED STANDARD BOX $35	MATCHING ROUND PLASTIC BOTTLE $15

163. bottle

164. front

164. back

164. HOLLY HOBBIE (GINGHAM CHECK RIM)				
AL	1980 – 1983	R: 2	EMBOSSED STANDARD BOX $35	MATCHING ROUND PLASTIC BOTTLE $15

165. front & bottle

165. back

165. HOMETOWN AIRPORT ARTIST: ED WEXLER				
KST	1960	BOX, R: 9 BOTTLE, R: 7	DOME BOX $1,500	MATCHING STEEL/GLASS BOTTLE $250

166. front

166. back & bottle

166. HONG KONG PHOOEY				
BASED ON THE HANNA-BARBERA TV CARTOON SERIES; ARTIST: NICK LoBIANCO				
KST	1975	R: 5	STANDARD BOX $75	MATCHING SQUARE PLASTIC BOTTLE $35

167. bottle

167. front

167. HOPALONG CASSIDY BOX w/CLOUD DECAL				
THE ONE THAT STARTED IT ALL! THE FIRST LICENSED TV CHARACTER BOX, CAME IN RED OR BLUE ENAMEL; ARTIST: BOB BURTON				
AL	1950 – 1951	R: 7	STANDARD BOX $220	MATCHING STEEL/GLASS BOTTLE $125; CAME WITH TWO DIFFERENT HANDLE-LESS CUPS; THIS IS THE RARER ONE

168. front

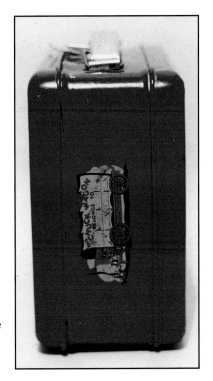

168. side

168. HOPALONG CASSIDY BOX w/SQUARE DECAL				
ARTIST: BOB BURTON				
THE SECOND ONE MADE, WITH A DIFFERENT DECAL SHAPE, ALSO CAME IN RED OR BLUE ENAMEL				
AL	1952 – 1953	R: 7	STANDARD BOX $220	SAME BOTTLE AS BOX #167

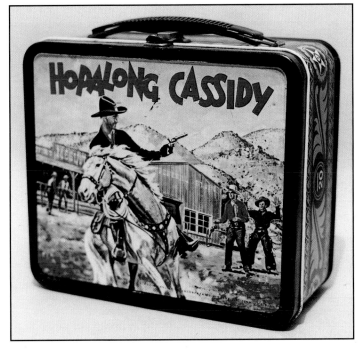

169. front

169. bottle

169. HOPALONG CASSIDY FULL FIGURE LITHO BOX				
ARTIST: BOB BURTON; SAME FRONT & BACK				
AL	1954	R: 7	STANDARD BOX $325	MATCHING STEEL/GLASS BOTTLE $175

170. bottle

171. bottle

170. HOT WHEELS
BASED ON MATTEL'S TOY CARS; ARTIST: RINALDO LEVERONE

KST	1968	R: 5	STANDARD BOX $100	MATCHING STEEL/GLASS BOTTLE $45
				MATCHING SQUARE PLASTIC BOTTLE $25

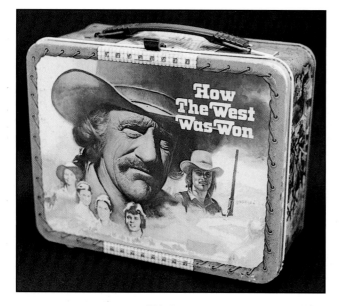

171. front

171. back

171. HOW THE WEST WAS WON
BASED ON THE TV SERIES STARRING JAMES ARNESS

KST	1979	R: 4	STANDARD BOX $75	MATCHING SQUARE PLASTIC BOTTLE $35 TWO KNOWN VERSIONS; ONE WITH RED LETTERING, ONE WITH BLUE

172. front

172. back

		172. HOWDY DOODY		
		BASED ON THE TV SERIES; ARTIST: MILT NEIL		
AD	1954	R: 8	STANDARD BOX $500	NO MATCHING BOTTLE MADE

173. front

173. back

173. bottle

		173. HUCKLEBERRY HOUND		
	BASED ON THE HANNA-BARBERA TV CARTOON SERIES; ATTRIBUTED TO ARTIST: ELMER LEHNHARDT			
AL	1961	R: 7	FLAT OR EMBOSSED STANDARD BOX $200	MATCHING STEEL/GLASS BOTTLE $100

174. front & bottle

174. back

174. INCREDIBLE HULK				
ARTIST: ELMER LEHNHARDT				
AL	1978	R: 4	EMBOSSED STANDARD BOX $75	MATCHING ROUND PLASTIC BOTTLE $35

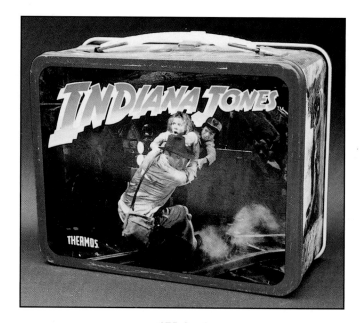

175. front

175. back

175. INDIANA JONES				
KST	1984	R: 3	STANDARD BOX $40	MATCHING SQUARE PLASTIC BOTTLE $20

176. front

175. bottle

176. INDIANA JONES & THE TEMPLE OF DOOM				
KST	1984	R: 3	EMBOSSED STANDARD BOX $40	SAME BOTTLE AS BOX #175

177. front

177. back

177. IT'S ABOUT TIME BASED OF THE TV SERIES; ARTIST: ELMER LEHNHARDT ANOTHER VERY POPULAR ITEM; A CONDITION 10 KIT (BOX & BOTTLE) COULD BE AS HIGH AS $1,500				
AL	1967	R: 8	DOME BOX $350	MATCHING STEEL/GLASS BOTTLE $200

119

178. front

178. JAMES BOND 007				
ARTIST: JOHN HENRY				
AL	1966	R: 8	EMBOSSED STANDARD BOX $350	MATCHING STEEL/GLASS BOTTLE $200

178. bottle

178. back

179. front & bottle

179. back

179. JET PATROL				
ARTISTS: BOB BURTON & ELMER LEHNHARDT				
AL	1957	R: 8	STANDARD BOX $350	MATCHING STEEL/GLASS BOTTLE $160

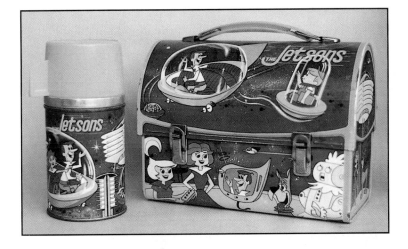

180. front & bottle

180. back

180. THE JETSONS				
BASED ON THE HANNA-BARBERA CARTOON TV SERIES; ARTISTS: BOB BURTON & ELMER LEHNHARDT				
AL	1963	R: 9	DOME BOX $1,200	MATCHING STEEL/GLASS BOTTLE $500

181. front

181. bottle

181. JULIA				
BASED ON THE TV SERIES STARRING DIAHANN CARROLL; ARTIST: NICK LoBIANCO				
KST	1969 – 1970	R: 5	STANDARD BOX $125	MATCHING STEEL/GLASS BOTTLE $60

181. back

182. bottle

182. JUNGLE BOOK				
BASED ON THE DISNEY MOVIE				
AL	1968 – 1969	R: 6	STANDARD BOX $100	MATCHING STEEL/GLASS BOTTLE $65

183. front

183. bottle

183. JUNIOR MISS				
THE FIRST IN A SERIES OF SIX; ARTIST: BOB BURTON; SAME FRONT & BACK				
AL	1956 – 1959	R: 6	STANDARD BOX $125	MATCHING STEEL/GLASS BOTTLE $70

184. front

184. bottle

184. bottle

184. JUNIOR MISS				
SAME FRONT & BACK				
AL	1966 – 1969	R: 5	STANDARD BOX $95	MATCHING STEEL/GLASS BOTTLE $45
				MATCHING ROUND PLASTIC BOTTLE w/GLASS INSERT $35

185. front

185. bottle

186. bottle

185. JUNIOR MISS SAME FRONT & BACK				
AL	1970 – 1971	R: 5	STANDARD BOX $95	ROUND PLASTIC BOTTLE w/GLASS INSERT $35

186. front

186. back

186. JUNIOR MISS				
AL	1973 – 1977	R: 5	STANDARD BOX $75	ROUND PLASTIC BOTTLE $30

187. front

187. back

187. JUNIOR MISS				
AL	1978 – 1980	R: 5	STANDARD BOX $80	MATCHING ROUND PLASTIC BOTTLE $30 (GIRL & DOG SITTING ON GRASS)

188. front & bottle

188. back

188. KELLOGG'S BREAKFAST CEREALS ARTIST: ELMER LEHNHARDT				
AL	1969	R: 7	EMBOSSED STANDARD BOX $250	MATCHING ROUND PLASTIC BOTTLE $75

189. front

189. back

189. KID POWER				
ARTIST: NICK LoBIANCO				
KST	1974 – 1975	R: 3	STANDARD BOX $55	MATCHING SQUARE PLASTIC BOTTLE $20

190. front

190. back

190. bottle

190. KING KONG				
BASED ON THE 1977 REMAKE OF THE MOVIE; ARTIST: DON HENRY				
KST	1977	R: 4	STANDARD BOX $80	MATCHING SQUARE PLASTIC BOTTLE $30

191. back

191. front & bottle

191. KNIGHT IN ARMOR				
UN	1959	R: 9	STANDARD BOX $1,000	MATCHING STEEL/GLASS BOTTLE $300

192. front & bottle

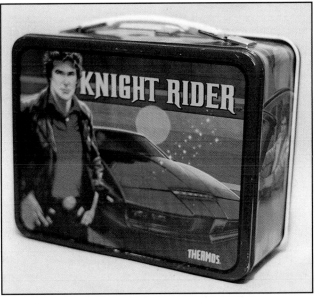

192. back

192. KNIGHT RIDER BASED ON THE TV SERIES STARRING DAVID HASSELHOFF; ARTIST: GENE LEMERY				
KST	1984 – 1985	R: 3	STANDARD BOX $45	MATCHING SQUARE PLASTIC BOTTLE $20

193. front

			193. KORG	
			193. KORG	
			BASED ON THE HANNA-BARBERA CARTOON TV SERIES; ARTIST: NICK LoBIANCO	
KST	1975	R: 4	STANDARD BOX $60	MATCHING SQUARE PLASTIC BOTTLE $40

193. back

193. bottle

194. front & bottle

194. back

194. THE KROFFT SUPERSHOW				
ARTIST: ELMER LEHNHARDT				
AL	1976	R: 5	EMBOSSED STANDARD BOX $100	MATCHING ROUND PLASTIC BOTTLE $45

195. front

195. back

195. KUNG FU				
BASED ON THE TV SERIES STARRING DAVID CARRADINE; ARTIST: NICK LoBIANCO				
KST	1974	R: 4	STANDARD BOX $100	MATCHING SQUARE PLASTIC BOTTLE $45

196. front

196. LAND OF THE GIANTS				
BASED ON THE TV SERIES; THE GIANT HEAD IS A SELF-PORTRAIT OF THE ARTIST: ELMER LEHNHARDT				
AL	1969 – 1970	R: 7	EMBOSSED STANDARD BOX $150	MATCHING ROUND PLASTIC BOTTLE $100

196. back

196. bottle

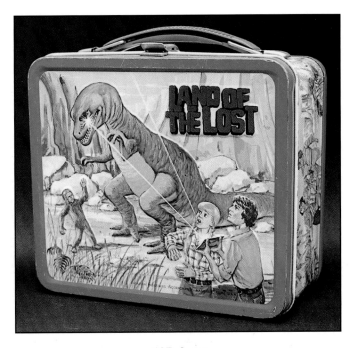

197. front

	*197. LAND OF THE LOST* BASED ON THE TV SERIES; ARTIST: ELMER LEHNHARDT
AL	1975	R: 5	EMBOSSED STANDARD BOX $125	MATCHING ROUND PLASTIC BOTTLE $50

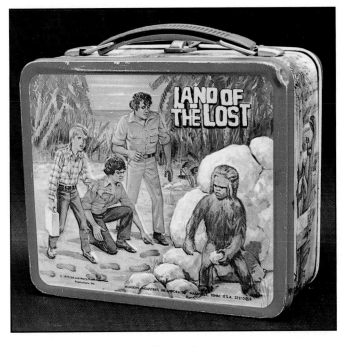

197. back

197. bottle

198. front & bottle

198. back

198. LAUGH-IN (NAZI HELMET)				
BASED ON THE TV SERIES				
AL	1968	R: 6	STANDARD BOX $135	MATCHING ROUND PLASTIC BOTTLE $65

199. front

199. back

199. THE LEGEND OF THE LONE RANGER				
AL	1980	R: 4	STANDARD BOX $75	MATCHING ROUND PLASTIC BOTTLE $30

200. front

200. LIDSVILLE				
BASED ON THE CARTOON SERIES; ARTIST: ELMER LEHNHARDT				
AL	1971	R: 6	STANDARD BOX $125	MATCHING ROUND PLASTIC BOTTLE $60

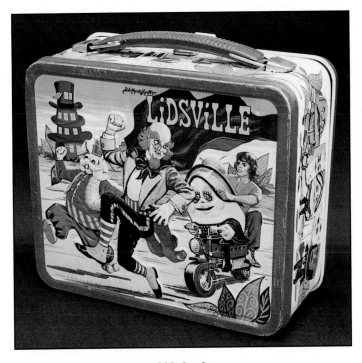

200. back

200. bottle

201. front

201. bottle

202. bottle

201. LITTLE DUTCH MISS				
SAME FRONT & BACK				
UN	1959	R: 6	STANDARD BOX $175	MATCHING STEEL/GLASS BOTTLE $75

202. front

202. back

202. LITTLE HOUSE ON THE PRAIRIE				
BASED ON THE TV SERIES STARRING MICHAEL LANDON; ARTIST: GENE LEMERY				
KST	1978	R: 5	STANDARD BOX $100	MATCHING SQUARE PLASTIC BOTTLE $45

203. front

203. back

203. LITTLE RED RIDING HOOD				
OA	1982 – 1984	R: 6	STANDARD BOX $145	NO MATCHING BOTTLE MADE

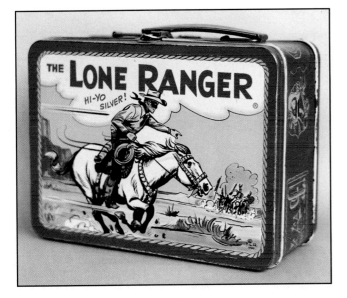

204. front

204. back

204. THE LONE RANGER (RED BAND)				
AD	1954	R: 8	STANDARD BOX $500	NO MATCHING BOTTLE MADE

205. front

205. bottle

			205. LOONEY TUNES (TV SET)	
AT	1959	R: 8	STANDARD BOX $300	MATCHING STEEL/GLASS BOTTLE $130

205. back

206. bottle

			206. LUDWIG VON DRAKE	
AL	1962	R: 7	STANDARD BOX $210	MATCHING STEEL/GLASS BOTTLE $120

207. Indian head Medallion

207. front

	**207. LUGGAGE PLAID**				
	SHOWING INDIAN HEAD MEDALLION, A CHARACTERISTIC FEATURE OF ADCO'S BOXES; SAME FRONT & BACK				
AD	1955	R: 7	STANDARD BOX $190		NO MATCHING BOTTLE MADE

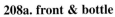

208a. front & bottle

208b. front & bottle

	**208. LUGGAGE TWEED**		
AT	1957 – 1963	R: 6	SAME FRONT & BACK
	A) MAROON STANDARD BOX $145	colspan=2	MATCHING STEEL/GLASS BOTTLE $50
	B) TAN STANDARD BOX $125	colspan=2	MATCHING STEEL/GLASS BOTTLE $50
	BLUE STANDARD BOX (NOT PICTURED) $155	colspan=2	MATCHING STEEL/GLASS BOTTLE $75

209. front

209. back

209. THE LUNCH MASTER				
ELECTRIC LUNCHBOX				
L&W LEBANON, OR	1950s	R: 9	TOOL BOX-STYLE DOME BOX $550	BOTTLE UNKNOWN

210. front

210. back

210. bottle

210. THE MAGIC OF LASSIE				
BASED ON THE TV SERIES				
KST	1978	R: 4	STANDARD BOX $70	MATCHING SQUARE PLASTIC BOTTLE $30

211. front & bottle

211. back

			211. THE MAN FROM U.N.C.L.E. BASED ON THE TV SERIES	
KST	1966	R: 7	STANDARD BOX $300	MATCHING STEEL/GLASS BOTTLE $110

212. front

212. back

212. bottle

			212. MARY POPPINS BASED ON THE DISNEY MOVIE	
AL	1965	R: 5	STANDARD BOX $100	MATCHING STEEL/GLASS BOTTLE $65

213. front & bottle

213. back

213. MASTERS OF THE UNIVERSE
ARTIST: BOB JONES

AL	1983	R: 2	EMBOSSED STANDARD BOX $25	MATCHING ROUND PLASTIC BOTTLE $15

214. front

214. back

214. MICKEY MOUSE & DONALD DUCK

AD	1954	BOX, R: 8 BOTTLE, R: 10	STANDARD BOX $450	MATCHING STEEL/GLASS BOTTLE $1,500

214. bottle

215. front

215. MICKEY MOUSE CLUB (YELLOW RIM)				
SERIES BEGAN IN 1955 WITH ANNETTE & FRIENDS, BUT BOX WAS MADE WHEN SHOW WAS SYNDICATED				
AL	1963 – 1967	R: 4	EMBOSSED STANDARD BOX $80	MATCHING ROUND PLASTIC BOTTLE $35

215. back

216. bottle

216. MICKEY MOUSE CLUB (WHITE RIM)				
AL	1976	R: 5	STANDARD BOX $90	MATCHING STEEL/GLASS BOTTLE $55

217. bottle

217. front

217. MICKEY MOUSE CLUB (RED RIM)				
AL	1977 – 1978	R: 4	STANDARD BOX $60	MATCHING ROUND PLASTIC BOTTLE $25

218. front

218. back

218. MICKEY MOUSE SKATING PARTY				
CHEINCO	1980s	R: 7	CARRY-ALL BOX $50	NO BOTTLE MADE

219. bottle

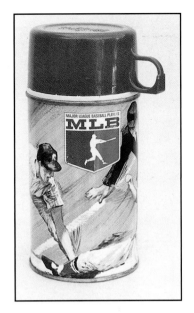

220. bottle

			219. MISS AMERICA A MISS AMERICA PAGEANT LICENSED PRODUCT; ARTIST: SALLY AUGUSTINI	
AL	1972	R: 4	EMBOSSED STANDARD BOX $75	MATCHING ROUND PLASTIC BOTTLE $55

			220. MLB BOX & BOTTLE ARE IDENTICAL TO "PLAY BALL" BOX EXCEPT FOR THE ADDITION OF THE MLB LOGO; ARTIST: NICK LoBIANCO	
KST	1968	R: 6	STANDARD BOX $100	MATCHING STEEL/GLASS BOTTLE $50

221. front

			221. MOD TULIPS SAME FRONT & BACK	
OA	1962	R: 7	DOME BOX $300	NO MATCHING BOTTLE MADE

222. front

222. bottle

222. THE MONROES				
BASED ON THE TV SERIES				
AL	1967	R: 6	STANDARD BOX $175	MATCHING STEEL/GLASS BOTTLE $120

223. front & bottle

223. back

223. MORK & MINDY				
BASED ON THE TV SERIES				
KST	1979	R: 3	STANDARD BOX $50	MATCHING SQUARE PLASTIC BOTTLE $25

224. front

224. MOSKOWITZ JAPAN AIR LINES				
©CHEWIE NEWGETT COMPANY	1974	R: 10	DOME BOX $750	NO BOTTLE KNOWN

225. front & bottle

225. back

225. MR. MERLIN BASED ON THE TV SERIES				
KST	1982	R: 2	STANDARD BOX $40	MATCHING SQUARE PLASTIC BOTTLE $20

226. back

226. front & bottle

226. THE MUNSTERS BASED ON THE TV SERIES				
KST	1965	R: 7	STANDARD BOX $400	MATCHING STEEL/GLASS BOTTLE $200

227. front

227. back

227. MUPPET BABIES				
KST	1985	R: 3	STANDARD BOX $40	MATCHING SQUARE PLASTIC BOTTLE $20

227. bottle

228. front

228. MUPPET MOVIE				
KST	1979	R: 4	STANDARD BOX $60	MATCHING SQUARE PLASTIC BOTTLE $20

228. back

229. front

229. back

229. THE MUPPET SHOW				
KST	1978	R: 3	STANDARD BOX $40	MATCHING SQUARE PLASTIC BOTTLE $15

230. front

230. back

230. bottle

230. THE MUPPETS (FOZZIE)				
KST	1979	R: 4	STANDARD BOX $50	MATCHING SQUARE PLASTIC BOTTLE $15

231. front

231. back

231. *THE MUPPETS (KERMIT)*				
KST	1979	R: 4	STANDARD BOX $50	SAME MUPPETS BOTTLE AS #230

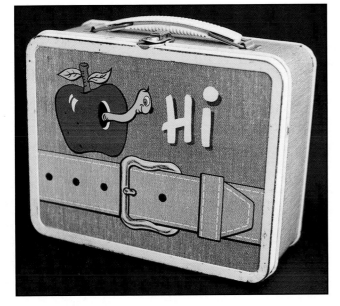

232. front

232. back

232. *MY LUNCH*				
OA	1974	R: 4	STANDARD BOX $55	NO MATCHING BOTTLE MADE

233. front

234. bottle

233. NANCY DREW MYSTERIES				
BASED ON THE TV SERIES STARRING PAMELA SUE MARTIN; SAME FRONT & BACK				
KST	1977	R: 4	STANDARD BOX $55	MATCHING SQUARE PLASTIC BOTTLE $25

234. front

234. back

234. NFL AMERICAN & NATIONAL CONFERENCES (GREEN BACKGROUND)			
UN	1962	R: 7	STANDARD BOX $200	MATCHING STEEL/GLASS BOTTLE $125

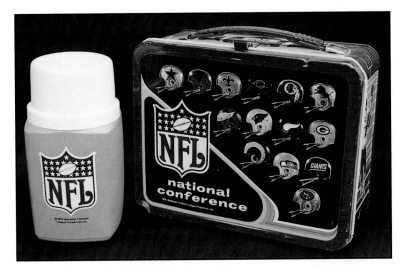

235. front & bottle

235. back

235. NFL NATIONAL & AMERICAN CONFERENCES (RED RIM)				
KST	1976	R: 4	STANDARD BOX $50	MATCHING SQUARE PLASTIC BOTTLE $15

236. front & bottle

236. back

236. NFL NATIONAL & AMERICAN CONFERENCES (YELLOW RIM)				
KST	1975	R: 4	STANDARD BOX $50	MATCHING SQUARE PLASTIC BOTTLE $15

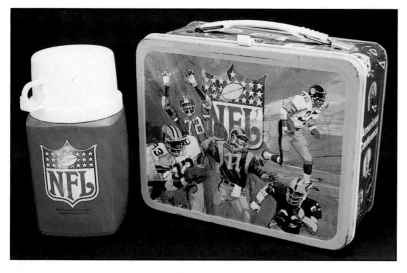

237. front & bottle

237. back

237. NFL NATIONAL & AMERICAN CONFERENCES (LIGHT BLUE RIM)				
KST	1978	R: 4	STANDARD BOX $50	MATCHING SQUARE PLASTIC BOTTLE $15

238. front

238. back

238. NFL QUARTERBACK				
AL	1964	R: 7	STANDARD BOX $160	MATCHING STEEL/GLASS BOTTLE $80

238. bottle

239. bottle

239. front

239. ORBIT					
ARTIST'S RENDERING OF *NATIONAL GEOGRAPHIC'S* HISTORIC PHOTO OF JOHN GLENN, FIRST AMERICAN TO ORBIT THE EARTH, WAS USED WITHOUT PERMISSION FROM THE MAGAZINE WHICH MADE KST CEASE PRODUCTION OF THE BOX.					
KST	1963	R: 7	STANDARD BOX $225	TALL MATCHING STEEL/GLASS BOTTLE $100	
				SHORT MATCHING STEEL/GLASS BOTTLE $75	

239. back & bottle

240. front

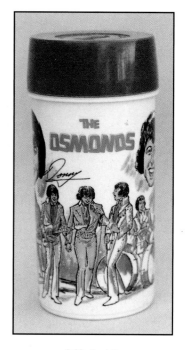

240. bottle

240. THE OSMONDS				
TELEVISION, CONCERT, AND RECORDING ARTISTS				
AL	1973	R: 4	STANDARD BOX $75	MATCHING ROUND PLASTIC BOTTLE $45

240. back

241. bottle

241. OUTDOOR SPORTS TALL STEEL/GLASS BOTTLE				
AT	1955	R: 6	BOTTLE $50	SOLD SEPARATELY

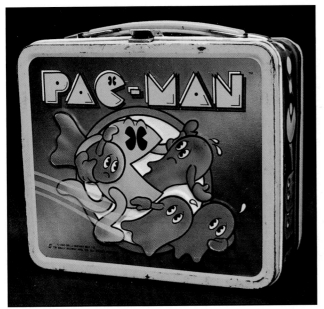

242. front

242. back

		242. PAC-MAN		
		BASED ON THE VIDEO GAME		
AL	1980	R: 3	STANDARD BOX $40	MATCHING ROUND PLASTIC BOTTLE $15

242. bottle

243. bottle

		243. PALADIN (HAVE GUN WILL TRAVEL)		
		BASED ON *HAVE GUN WILL TRAVEL*, THE TV SERIES; PALADIN WAS THE CHARACTER RICHARD BOONE PLAYED; ARTIST: BOB BURTON		
AL	1960	R: 7	STANDARD BOX $300	MATCHING STEEL/GLASS BOTTLE $160

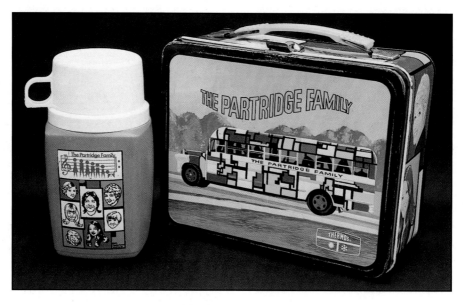

244. front & bottle

	***244. THE PARTRIDGE FAMILY*** BASED ON THE TV SERIES FEATURING SHIRLEY JONES AND HER REAL-LIFE SON, DAVID CASSIDY; ARTIST: NICK LoBIANCO

KST	1971	R: 5	STANDARD BOX $100	MATCHING SQUARE PLASTIC BOTTLE $30
				MATCHING STEEL/GLASS BOTTLE $50

244. bottle   **245. bottle**

	***245. PATHFINDER***

UN	1959	R: 8	STANDARD BOX $525	MATCHING STEEL/GLASS BOTTLE $200
				SAME BOTTLE w/COMPASS ON CUP $240

246. front

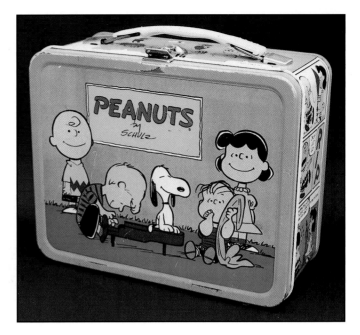

247. front

246. PATRIOTIC				
AKA "FIFE & DRUM;" SAME FRONT & BACK				
OA	1975	R: 4	STANDARD BOX $50	NO MATCHING BOTTLE MADE

247. back

247. bottle

247. PEANUTS (ORANGE RIM)				
BASED ON THE COMIC STRIP AND TV SPECIALS; ARTIST: NICK LoBIANCO				
KST	1973	R: 5	STANDARD BOX $75	MATCHING STEEL/GLASS BOTTLE $35

248. front

248. back

248. PEANUTS (RED BACKGROUND) ARTIST: NICK LoBIANCO				
KST	1976	R: 4	STANDARD BOX $65	MATCHING RED SQUARE PLASTIC BOTTLE w/SNOOPY DECAL $20

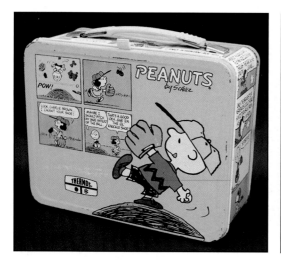

249. front

249. back

249. bottle

249. PEANUTS (GREEN BAND) ARTIST: NICK LoBIANCO				
KST	1980	R: 4	STANDARD BOX $55	MATCHING SQUARE PLASTIC BOTTLE $20

250. bottle

251. front

250. PEBBLES & BAMM BAMM				
BASED ON THE TWO OF THE HANNA-BARBERA FLINTSTONES TV SERIES CHARACTERS; ARTIST: ELMER LEHNHARDT				
AL	1971	R: 4	STANDARD BOX $75	MATCHING ROUND PLASTIC BOTTLE $50

251. PENNANTS				
OA	1950 – 1954	R: 5	CARRY-ALL BOX $35	CONTAINED A PIE TRAY; NO BOTTLE MADE

252. front

252. back

252. bottle

252. PETE'S DRAGON				
BASED ON THE DISNEY MOVIE; ARTIST: BEVERLY BURGE				
AL	1978	R: 4	EMBOSSED STANDARD BOX $55	MATCHING ROUND PLASTIC BOTTLE $25

253. front

253. back

			253. PETER PAN	
			BASED ON THE DISNEY MOVIE	
AL	1969	R: 5	EMBOSSED STANDARD BOX $90	MATCHING ROUND PLASTIC BOTTLE $30

254. front

254. bottle

			254. PETS AND PALS	
KST	1961	R: 6	STANDARD BOX $100	MATCHING STEEL/GLASS BOTTLE $45 (ONE OF THREE BOTTLES MADE FOR THIS BOX)

255. front

255. back

255. PIGS IN SPACE				
BASED ON THE MOVIE FEATURING JIM HENSON'S MUPPETS CHARACTERS				
KST	1977	R: 3	STANDARD BOX $40	MATCHING SQUARE PLASTIC BOTTLE $20

256. front

256. back

256. bottle

256. PINK PANTHER AND SONS				
BASED ON THE TV SERIES CARTOON SHOW, A RARE VERSION OF THE BOX WITH THE ART ON THE BACK PRINTED UPSIDE DOWN				
KST	1984	R: 9 (R: 3 IF RIGHT SIDE UP)	STANDARD BOX AS SHOWN $75	MATCHING SQUARE PLASTIC BOTTLE $20
			SAME BUT PRINTED RIGHT SIDE UP $40	

257. front & bottle

257. PINOCCHIO			
BASED ON THE DISNEY MOVIE			

AL	1971	R: 5	STANDARD BOX $100	MATCHING ROUND PLASTIC BOTTLE $50

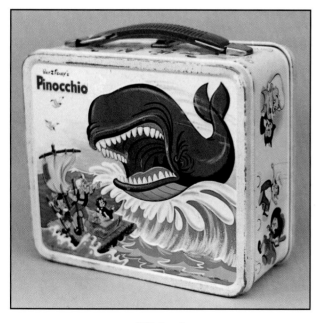

257. back

258. front

258. PLAID CARRY-ALL			
SAME FRONT & BACK			

OA	1950s	R: 5	BOX $50	NO BOTTLE MADE

259. bottle

259. back

259. PLAID				
SAME FRONT & BACK				
AL	1955	R: 5	STANDARD BOX $65	MATCHING STEEL/GLASS BOTTLE $30

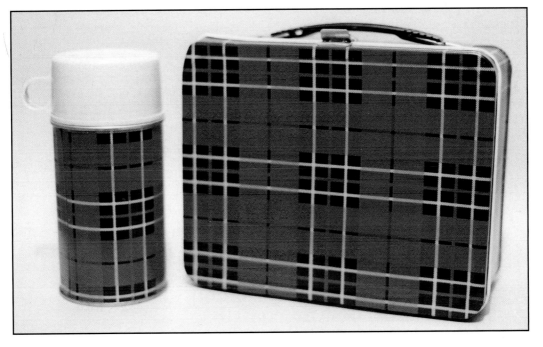

260. front & bottle

260. PLAID (McPHERSON)				
SAME FRONT & BACK				
KST	1964	R: 4	STANDARD BOX $45	MATCHING STEEL/GLASS BOTTLE $25

261. front & bottle

262. front

			261. PLAID (RED BAND) IDENTICAL PLAID BOX ALSO MADE WITH GREEN BAND; SAME FRONT & BACK	
AT	1960	R: 6	STANDARD BOX $90	MATCHING STEEL/GLASS BOTTLE $45

			262. PLAID SAME FRONT & BACK	
OA	1964	R: 5	STANDARD BOX $35	NO MATCHING BOTTLE MADE

263. front

			263. PLAID SAME FRONT & BACK	
OA	1964 – 1971	R: 5	STANDARD BOX $70	NO MATCHING BOTTLE MADE

264. front & bottle

264. PLAID				
SAME FRONT & BACK				
KST	1959	R: 5	STANDARD BOX $100	MATCHING STEEL/GLASS BOTTLE $65

265. front

265. PLAID (RED, GREEN & YELLOW DIAGONAL)				
SAME FRONT & BACK				
KST	1958	R: 8	DOME BOX $250	MATCHING TALL STEEL/GLASS BOTTLE $100

266. front

266. PLAID (RED & WHITE DIAGONAL)			
SAME FRONT & BACK			

KST	1960	R: 8	DOME BOX $250	BOTTLE UNKNOWN

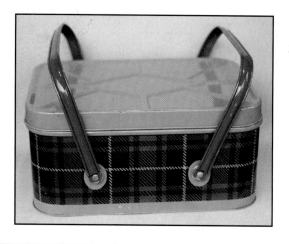

267. front

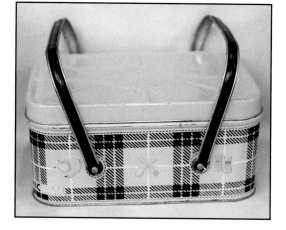

268. front

267. PLAID PICNIC BASKET				
SAME FRONT & BACK				

UNK (PROBABLY NASCO)	1950s – 1960s	R: 5	LARGE CARRY-ALL BASKET $35	BOTTLE UNKNOWN

268. PLAID "PICNIC RYTE" PICNIC BASKET				
SAME FRONT & BACK				

NASCO	1950s – 1960s	R: 7	LARGE CARRY-ALL BASKET $40	BOTTLE UNKNOWN

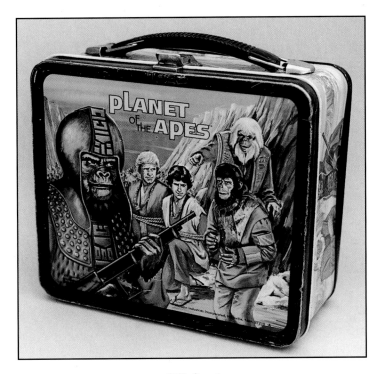

269. front

269. PLANET OF THE APES				
BASED ON THE SERIES OF MOVIES; ARTIST: ELMER LEHNHARDT				
AL	1974	R: 7	EMBOSSED STANDARD BOX $125	MATCHING ROUND PLASTIC BOTTLE $50

269. bottle

269. back

270. front

270. PLAY BALL (WITH MAGNETIC GAME ON BACK)				
IDENTICAL TO MLB BOX & BOTTLE BUT LACKING THE MLB LOGO; ARTIST: NICK LoBIANCO				
KST	1969	R: 6	STANDARD BOX $100	MATCHING STEEL/GLASS BOTTLE $50

270. back

270. bottle

271. front

271. POLLY PAL				
KST	1975	R: 3	STANDARD BOX $40	MATCHING ROUND PLASTIC BOTTLE $15

271. back

271. bottle

272. front

272. back

			272. POPEYE	
			BASED ON THE COMICS AND CARTOONS	
UN	1962	BOX, R: 9 BOTTLE, R: 10	STANDARD BOX $750	MATCHING STEEL/GLASS BOTTLE $1,000

273. front

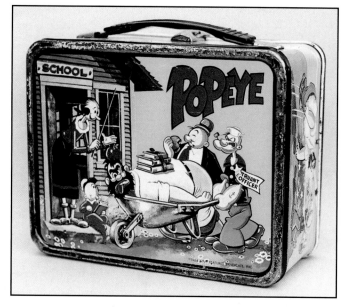

273. back

			273. POPEYE	
KST	1964	R: 6	STANDARD BOX $130	MATCHING STEEL/GLASS BOTTLE $65

273. bottle

274. back, bottle & cup

274. POPEYE				
AL	1980	R: 4	STANDARD BOX $60	MATCHING ROUND PLASTIC BOTTLE & TUMBLER $30

274. front

275. front

275. back

275. POPPLES				
BASED ON THE TV CARTOON SERIES				
AL	1986	R: 2	STANDARD BOX $30	MATCHING ROUND PLASTIC BOTTLE $10

276. front

276. back

276. PORKY'S LUNCH WAGON				
THE MOST BELOVED WARNER BROS. CARTOON CHARACTERS				
AT	1959	R: 8	DOME BOX $500	MATCHING STEEL/GLASS BOTTLE $200

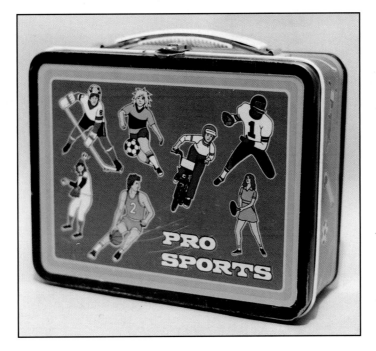

277. front

277. PRO SPORTS SAME FRONT & BACK				
OA	1980	R: 5	STANDARD BOX $80	NO MATCHING BOTTLE MADE

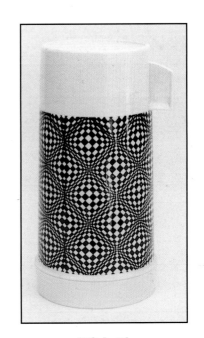

278. bottle

278. front

278. PSYCHEDELIC SAME FRONT & BACK				
AL	1969	R: 8	DOME BOX $370	MATCHING ROUND PLASTIC BOTTLE $90

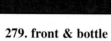

279. front & bottle

279. back

279. RACING WHEELS				
KST	1977	R: 4	STANDARD BOX $60	MATCHING SQUARE PLASTIC BOTTLE $30 (ORIGINALLY HAD WHITE CUP)

280. front

280. back

280. bottle

280. RAGGEDY ANN STANDARD BOX				
AL	1973	R: 3	STANDARD BOX $40	MATCHING SQUARE PLASTIC BOTTLE $15

281. bottle

281. front

282. bottle

281. RAMBO				
THE LAST OF THE STEEL BOXES MADE; HAD SAME ART BACK & FRONT				
KST	1985	R: 2	STANDARD BOX $25	MATCHING ROUND PLASTIC BOTTLE $10

282. THE RAT PATROL				
BASED ON THE TV SERIES; ARTIST: ELMER LEHNHARDT				
AL	1967	R: 6	STANDARD BOX $150	MATCHING STEEL/GLASS BOTTLE $75

282. front

282. back

283. front

283. back

283. RECYCLE WITH ROSCOE				
MADE OF RECYCLED AMERICAN STEEL				
ENGLAND	1990	R: 5	STANDARD BOX $110	BOTTLE UNKNOWN

284. front

284. RED AND GRAY				
AL	1950s	R: 4	STANDARD BOX $25	GENERIC STEEL/GLASS BOTTLE $20

285. front

285. back

285. RED BARN (CLOSED DOORS)				
AT	1957	R: 5	DOME BOX $120	GENERIC HOLTEMP STEEL/GLASS BOTTLE $20

286. back

286. front

286. RED BARN (OPEN DOORS)				
AT	1958	R: 5	DOME BOX $110	MATCHING STEEL/GLASS BOTTLE $40

177

287. front

287. back

			287. RED BARN (CUTESIE)	
KST	1971	R: 5	DOME BOX $110	MATCHING STEEL/GLASS BOTTLE $40

288. front

288. back

288. bottle

			288. THE RESCUERS	
			BASED ON THE DISNEY MOVIE	
AL	1977	R: 5	STANDARD BOX $100	MATCHING ROUND PLASTIC BOTTLE $30

289. front

289. RETURN OF THE JEDI				
BASED ON THE MOVIE; ARTIST: GENE LEMERY				
KST	1983	R: 4	STANDARD BOX $65	MATCHING SQUARE PLASTIC BOTTLE $15

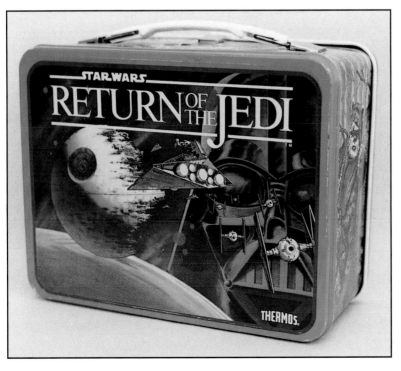

289. back

289. bottle

290. front & bottle

290. back

290. THE RIFLEMAN				
BASED ON THE TV SERIES STARRING CHUCK CONNORS; ARTIST: ELMER LEHNHARDT				
AL	1961	R: 8	STANDARD BOX $400	MATCHING STEEL/GLASS BOTTLE $155

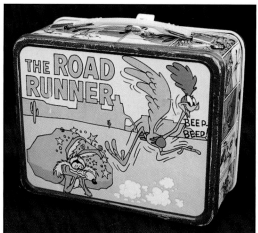

291. front

291. back

291. bottle

291. ROAD RUNNER				
CAME WITH PURPLE OR LAVENDER RIM; VALUE SAME FOR EACH; BASED ON THE CARTOONS; ARTIST: NICK LoBIANCO				
KST	1970	R: 4	STANDARD BOX $65	MATCHING STEEL/GLASS BOTTLE $45
				MATCHING SQUARE PLASTIC BOTTLE $25

292. front & bottle

292. ROBIN HOOD				
CARRIES THE GOOD HOUSEKEEPING SEAL OF APPROVAL; ARTIST: BOB BURTON				
AL	1965	R: 7	STANDARD BOX $225	MATCHING STEEL/GLASS BOTTLE $140

292. back

292. side

293. front

293. RONALD McDONALD SHERIFF OF CACTUS CANYON				
ARTIST: BRUCE MATTHEWS				
AL	1982	R: 3	EMBOSSED STANDARD BOX $45	MATCHING ROUND PLASTIC BOTTLE $15

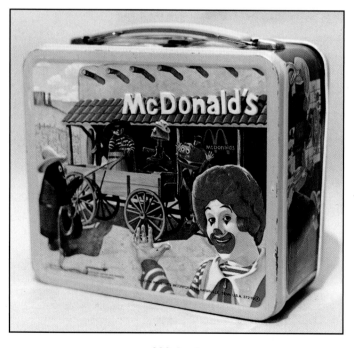

293. back

293. bottle

294. front

294. ROSE PETAL PLACE				
AL	1973	R: 3	STANDARD BOX $50	MATCHING ROUND PLASTIC BOTTLE $15

294. back

294. bottle

295. front

295. ROUGH RIDER				
ARTIST: ELMER LEHNHARDT				
AL	1973	R: 4	EMBOSSED STANDARD BOX $70	MATCHING ROUND PLASTIC BOTTLE $40 TWO SLIGHTLY DIFFERENT VERSIONS MADE: THE ONE SHOWN WITH HANDLED CUP, AND ANOTHER WITH OPEN HANDLED CUP AND GREEN BASE

295. back

295. bottle

296. front

	*296. ROY ROGERS (BLUE BAND)* ARTIST: ED WEXLER			

AT	1954	R: 7	STANDARD BOX $185	MATCHING STEEL/GLASS BOTTLE $150 TWO DIFFERENT BOTTLES WERE MADE: THE ONE SHOWN HERE WITH ART OF ROY, DALE, TRIGGER, AND BULLET; ANOTHER WITH ALL-OVER WOOD GRAIN PATTERN; VALUES SAME FOR EITHER

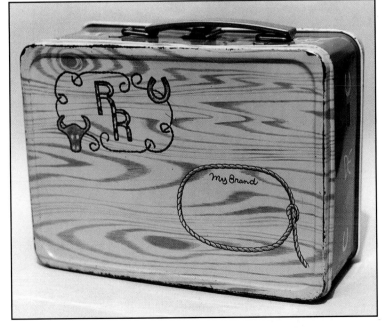

296. back

296. bottle

297. front

297. ROY ROGERS (BLUE BAND)				
EIGHT SCENES ON BACK OF BOX; ARTIST: ED WEXLER				
AT	1955	R: 7	STANDARD BOX $180	MATCHING STEEL/GLASS HOLTEMP $150

297. back

297. bottle

298. front

298. back

298. ROY ROGERS ON RAIL (BLUE BAND)				
ALSO MADE w/RED BAND; VALUE SAME FOR EITHER; ARTIST: ED WEXLER				
AT	1957	R: 7	STANDARD BOX $180	MATCHING STEEL/GLASS BOTTLE $165 SAME FIGURAL ART AS BOTTLE #297 BUT WITH YELLOW SKY

299. front & bottle

299. SADDLEBAG				
SAME ART FRONT AND BACK				
KST	1977	R: 6	STANDARD BOX $140	GENERIC SQUARE PLASTIC BOTTLE $40

300. front

			300. SATELLITE BOX MADE IN NARROW AND WIDE VERSIONS; MFG NAME CHANGE DUE TO KING SEELY BUYING AMERICAN THERMOS
AT	1958	R: 6	NARROW BOX $150
KST	1960	R: 6	WIDE BOX $140
AT	1958 – 1962	R: 6	MATCHING STEEL/GLASS BOTTLE (SAME ONE AS ASTRONAUT DOME) $80

300. back

300. bottle

301. front

301. back

			301. SCHOOL DAYS	
OA	1960	R: 6	STANDARD BOX $160	NO MATCHING BOTTLE MADE

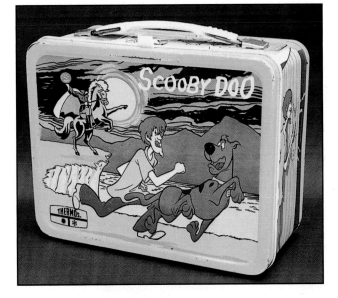

302. front

302. back

			302. SCOOBY DOO (YELLOW RIM)	
			BASED ON THE HANNA-BARBERA CARTOON TV SERIES; MADE WITH BOTH ORANGE AND YELLOW RIMS	
KST	1973 – 1976	R: 4	STANDARD BOX $75	MATCHING SQUARE PLASTIC BOTTLE $35

303. bottle

303. front

	**303. SECRET AGENT** HAS SPIN GAME ON BACK; ARTIST: NICK LoBIANCO			
KST	1968	R: 5	STANDARD BOX $135	MATCHING STEEL/GLASS BOTTLE $50

304. front

304. back

304. bottle

	**304. THE SECRET OF NIMH** BASED ON THE DISNEY MOVIE; ARTIST: BOB JONES			
AL	1982	R: 3	STANDARD BOX $55	MATCHING ROUND PLASTIC BOTTLE $20

305. front

305. SECRET WARS				
THE SECOND KIT BASED ON MARVEL COMICS CHARACTERS				
AL	1984	R: 5	STANDARD BOX $70	MATCHING ROUND PLASTIC BOTTLE $30

305. bottle

305. back

306. front

306. back

306. SEE AMERICA				
ACTUALLY CALLED "TRAVELER" BY OHIO ART IN THEIR 1972 CATALOG				
OA	1972	R: 5	STANDARD BOX $75	NO MATCHING BOTTLE MADE

307. front

307. back

307. bottle

307. SESAME STREET (GREEN RIM)				
BASED ON THE TV CARTOON SERIES; ARTIST: BEVERLY BURGE				
AL	1979	R: 3	EMBOSSED STANDARD BOX $45	MATCHING ROUND PLASTIC BOTTLE $15

308. front

	**308. SESAME STREET (YELLOW RIM)** ARTIST: BEVERLY BURGE
AL	1983	R: 3	EMBOSSED STANDARD BOX $40	MATCHING ROUND PLASTIC BOTTLE $15

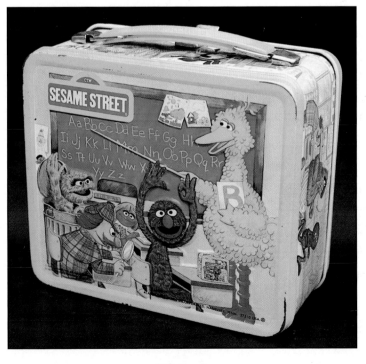

308. back

308. bottle

309. front

309. back

	**309. SIGMOND & THE SEA MONSTERS** BASED ON THE TV CARTOON SERIES; ARTIST: ANN CUMMINGS
AL	1974	R: 6	STANDARD BOX $125	MATCHING ROUND PLASTIC BOTTLE $50

310. bottle

311. bottle

	**310. SIX MILLION DOLLAR MAN** BASED ON THE TV SERIES STARRING LEE MAJORS; FRONT ART IS STEVE'S DISEMBODIED HEAD; ARTIST: ELMER LEHNHARDT
AL	1974	R: 4	STANDARD BOX $75	MATCHING ROUND PLASTIC BOTTLE $35

	**311. SIX MILLION DOLLAR MAN** BOX FRONT ART IS STEVE PUNCHING THROUGH A WALL; ARTIST: ELMER LEHNHARDT
AL	1978	R: 4	STANDARD BOX $75	MATCHING ROUND PLASTIC BOTTLE $35

312. front

312. THE SKATEBOARDER				
AL	1977 – 1978	R: 4	STANDARD BOX $70	MATCHING ROUND PLASTIC BOTTLE $30

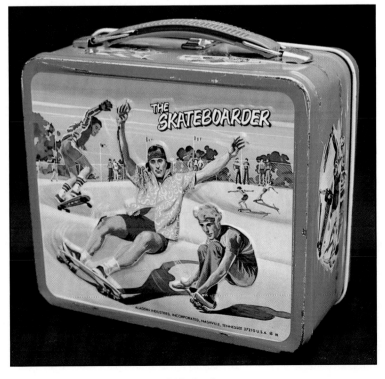

312. back

312. bottle

313. front

313. back

313. SLEEPING BEAUTY				
GSW, CANADA	1972	R: 8	CARRY-ALL BOX $475	NO BOTTLE MADE

314a. front

314a. back

314a. SNOOPY HOLDING BLUE CUP				
KST	1972	R: 9	DOME BOX $300	SAME BOTTLE AS RED CUP BOX #314B

314b. front

314b. bottle

			314b. SNOOPY HOLDING RED CUP	
KST	1970	R: 3	DOME BOX $100	MATCHING STEEL/GLASS BOTTLE $45
				YELLOW PLASTIC "DOG HOUSE" BOTTLE w/RED OR WHITE CUP $30

315. front

315. bottle

			315. SNOW WHITE (ORANGE RIM) BASED ON THE DISNEY MOVIE; ARTIST: ANN CUMMINGS	
AL	1975	R: 4	STANDARD BOX $65	MATCHING ROUND PLASTIC BOTTLE $30

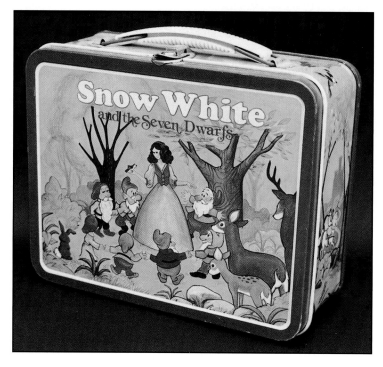

316. front

316. SNOW WHITE (PURPLE RIM)				
CAME EITHER WITH MAGNETIC GAME ON BACK OR WITH REPEAT OF FRONT ART ON BACK				
OA	1977	R: 4	STANDARD BOX WITH GAME $70	NO MATCHING BOTTLE MADE
OA	1980	R: 4	STANDARD BOX WITHOUT GAME $70	NO MATCHING BOTTLE MADE

317. front

317. back

317. SPACE: 1999				
BASED ON THE TV SERIES; ARTIST: ED WEXLER				
KST	1976	R: 4	STANDARD BOX $70	MATCHING SQUARE PLASTIC BOTTLE $30

318. front

318. SPACE SHUTTLE ORBITER ENTERPRISE				
ENTERPRISE WAS AMERICA'S FIRST SPACE SHUTTLE ORBITER; IT WAS SUPPOSED TO BE CALLED CONSTITUTION, BUT A WRITE-IN CAMPAIGN CONVINCED NASA TO CHANGE THE NAME; ARTIST: DON HENRY				
KST	1977	R: 5	STANDARD BOX $85	MATCHING SQUARE PLASTIC BOTTLE $45 DECAL CAME IN AT LEAST TWO DIFFERENT COLORS

318. back

318. bottle

319. front

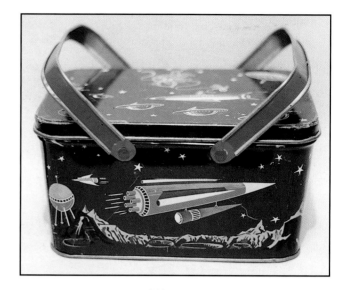

319. back

319. SPACE TRAVEL				
DECOWARE	1940s	R: 7	CARRY-ALL BOX $260	CONTAINED PIE TRAY; NO BOTTLE MADE

320. front

320. back

320. SPIDERMAN & HULK/CAPTAIN AMERICA ANOTHER MARVEL COMICS KIT				
AL	1980	R: 4	STANDARD BOX $60	MATCHING ROUND PLASTIC BOTTLE $20

321. front

321. back

321. SPORT GOOFY
BASED ON THE DISNEY CHARACTER; ARTIST: BOB JONES

AL	1983	R: 4	STANDARD BOX $55	MATCHING ROUND PLASTIC BOTTLE $20

322a. back & bottle

322b. front

322c. front

322. SPORT SKWIRTS
BOX CAME IN FOUR DIFFERENT VERSIONS;
ONE OF THE FEW OHIO ART BOXES SOLD WITH BOTTLES IN SOME MARKETS

OA	1982 – 1984	R: 3	A) SALLY SERVE/WILLIE DRIBBLE $45	GENERIC PLASTIC $15
OA	1982– 1984	R: 3	B) JIMMY BLOOPER/FRANKIE FUMBLE $45	BOTTLE UNKNOWN
OA	1982 – 1984	R: 3	C) FREDDIE FACEOFF/WOODIE SCORE $45	BOTTLE UNKNOWN
OA	1982 – 1984	R: 4	BOX w/FOUR CHARACTERS (NOT PICTURED) $55	BOTTLE UNKNOWN

323.

323. SPORTS (OVAL) SAME FRONT & BACK				
OA	1931	R: 7	CARRY-ALL BOX $110	NO BOTTLE MADE

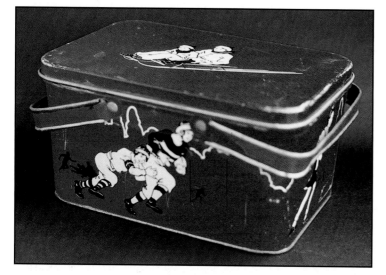

324. front

324. back

324. SPORTS (RECTANGULAR)				
DECO	1931	R: 7	CARRY-ALL BOX $110	NO BOTTLE MADE

325. front

325. SPORTS AFIELD				
SHOWING STAR MEDALLION, A FEATURE ON SOME OHIO ART BOXES				
OA	1957	R: 6	STANDARD BOX $150	NO MATCHING BOTTLE MADE

325. back

325. band

326. front & bottle

326. STAR TREK				
BASED ON THE TV SERIES; ARTISTS: BOB BURTON & ELMER LEHNHARDT				
AL	1968	R: 8	DOME BOX $1,000	MATCHING STEEL/GLASS BOTTLE $500

326. back

327. back

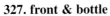

327. front & bottle

328. bottle

327. *STAR TREK THE MOTION PICTURE* ARTIST: GENE LEMERY				
KST	1980	R: 6	STANDARD BOX $200	MATCHING SQUARE PLASTIC BOTTLE $75

328. front

328. back

328. *STAR WARS (STARS ON BAND)* ARTIST: DON HENRY				
KST	1977	R: 3	STANDARD BOX $75	MATCHING SQUARE PLASTIC BOTTLE $30

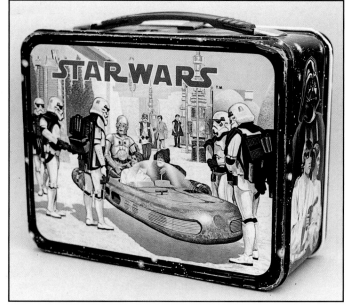

329. front

329. back

329. STAR WARS (CHARACTERS ON BAND)				
ARTIST: DON HENRY				
KST	1978	R: 4	STANDARD BOX $75	SAME BOTTLE AS STARS ON BAND BOX #328

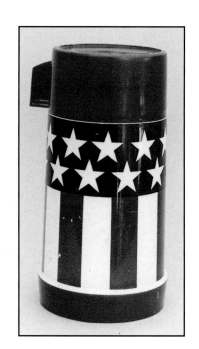

330. bottle

330. front

330. STARS & STRIPES				
SAME FRONT & BACK				
AL	1970	R: 5	DOME BOX $90	MATCHING ROUND PLASTIC BOTTLE $30

331. front & bottle

331. back

	**331. STEVE CANYON** THE COMIC STRIP BECAME A TV SERIES IN 1958; BOX BASED ON SERIES; ARTIST: MILT CANIFF
AL	1959	R: 7	STANDARD BOX $300	MATCHING STEEL/GLASS BOTTLE $155

332. front

332. back

332. bottle

	**332. STRAWBERRY SHORTCAKE (STRAWBERRY HOUSE)**
AL	1980	R: 2	STANDARD BOX $25	MATCHING ROUND PLASTIC BOTTLE $10

333. front

333. back

333. bottle

334. front

334. bottle

334. back

			333. STRAWBERRY SHORTCAKE (STRAWBERRY STAND)	
AL	1980	R: 2	STANDARD BOX $25	MATCHING ROUND PLASTIC BOTTLE $10

			334. STREET HAWK BASED ON THE TV SERIES; ARTIST: ELMER LEHNHARDT	
AL	1985	R: 6	EMBOSSED STANDARD BOX $165	MATCHING ROUND PLASTIC BOTTLE $75

335. front

335. bottle

335. SUBMARINE				
KST	1960	R: 5	STANDARD BOX $110	MATCHING STEEL/GLASS BOTTLE $65

336. bottles

336. bottom detail

336. SUNFLOWER BOTTLES				
SHANGHAI, CHINA	UNK	R: 7	SHOWING DETAIL OF CUP	STEEL/GLASS BOTTLES $30 EACH

337. front

337. back

			337. SUPER FRIENDS	
AL	1977 – 1979	R: 5	EMBOSSED STANDARD BOX $80	MATCHING ROUND PLASTIC BOTTLE $35

337. bottle

338. front

338. back

			338. SUPER POWERS	
AL	1983	R: 5	EMBOSSED STANDARD BOX $80	MATCHING ROUND PLASTIC BOTTLE $35

339. front & bottle

339. back

339. SUPERCAR ARTIST: WALLY WOOD				
UN	1962	R: 7	STANDARD BOX $350	MATCHING STEEL/GLASS BOTTLE $150

340. front

340. back

340. SUPERMAN ARTIST: WAYNE BORING				
UN	1954	R: 8	STANDARD BOX $1,000	NO MATCHING BOTTLE MADE

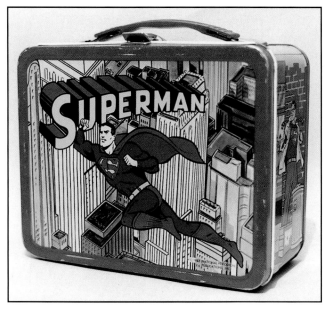

341. front

341. back

	***341. SUPERMAN*** ARTIST: NICK LoBIANCO
KST	1967	R: 6	STANDARD BOX $160	MATCHING STEEL/GLASS BOTTLE $80

342. front & bottle

341. bottle

342. back

	***342. SUPERMAN*** BASED ON THE MOVIE
AL	1978	R: 4	EMBOSSED STANDARD BOX $75	MATCHING ROUND PLASTIC BOTTLE $35

343. bottle

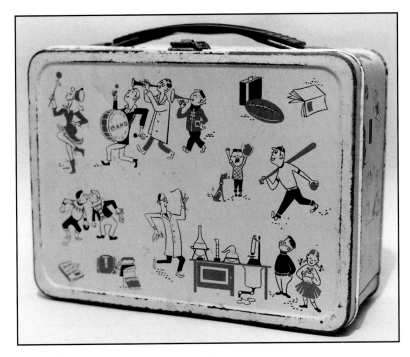

344. front

343. TARZAN				
ARTIST: JOHN HENRY				
AL	1966	R: 5	EMBOSSED STANDARD BOX $135	MATCHING STEEL/GLASS BOTTLE $75

344. back

344. TEENAGER				
AT	1957	R: 6	STANDARD BOX $100	GENERIC STEEL/GLASS BOTTLE $20

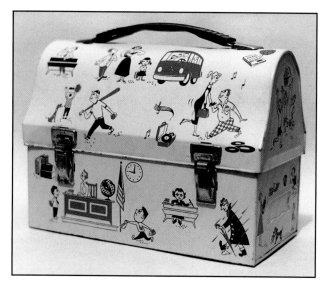

345. front

345. back

345. TEENAGER				
AT	1957	R: 6	DOME BOX $150	GENERIC STEEL/GLASS BOTTLE $20

346. front

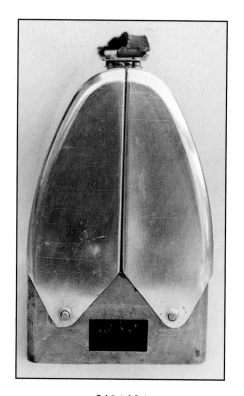

346 (side)

346. THERMETTE HOT LUNCH				
ELECTRIC BOX WITH PIE TRAY				
UNK	19	R: 10	DOME BOX $550	BOTTLE UNKNOWN

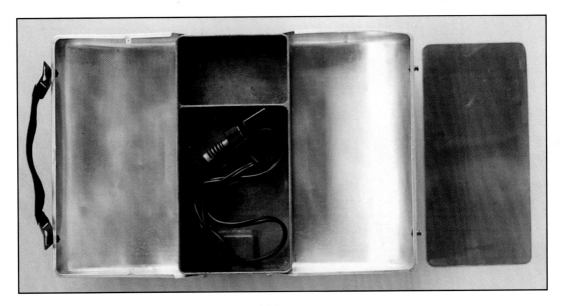

346. open

347. THREE LITTLE PIGS				
ONE OF A FEW KNOWN OHIO ART BOXES SOLD WITH BOTTLES IN SOME MARKETS				
OA	1982	R: 5	STANDARD BOX $80	GENERIC PLASTIC BOTTLE MADE IN TAIWAN $10

347. front

347. back

348. front

348. back

348. bottle

			348. THUNDERCATS ARTIST: DAN HOSSE	
AL	1985	R: 3	EMBOSSED STANDARD BOX $40	MATCHING ROUND PLASTIC BOTTLE $15

349. front

349. back

			349. TOM CORBETT SPACE CADET (DECAL) CAME IN RED OR BLUE ENAMEL w/SAME DECAL; ARTIST: BOB BURTON	
AL	1952	R: 7	STANDARD BOX $275	SAME BOTTLE AS #350 BUT WITH RED CAP $125

350. front

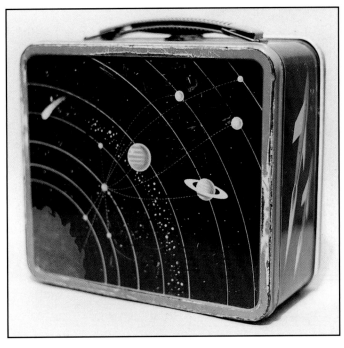

350. back

350. TOM CORBETT SPACE CADET (FULL LITHO BOX)				
TWO VERSIONS MADE: ONE WITH A LEGEND TO THE MAP OF THE STARS ON THE BACK, ONE WITHOUT THE LEGEND; ARTIST: BOB BURTON				
AL	1954	R: 8	STANDARD BOX w/LEGEND $450	MATCHING STEEL/GLASS BOTTLE $125
AL	1954	R: 8	STANDARD BOX wo/LEGEND $450	

350. legend

350. bottle

351. front

351. back

351. TRACK KING				
OK	1975	R: 7	STANDARD BOX $300	MATCHING STEEL/GLASS BOTTLE $200

352. front

353. front

352. TRAIN				
DECO	1930s	R: 5	CARRY-ALL BOX $125	NO BOTTLE MADE

353. TRANSPORTATION				
OA	1930s	R: 5	CARRY-ALL BOX $125	NO BOTTLE MADE

354. bottle

355. front

354. TRANSFORMERS				
BASED ON TOYS AND LATER TV SERIES; ART FROM HASBRO, THE LICENSER				
AL	1986	R: 3	STANDARD BOX $35	MATCHING ROUND PLASTIC BOTTLE $10

355. TRAVELER (BLUE)				
OA	1962	R: 5	STANDARD BOX $130	NO BOTTLE MADE

356. front

356. TRAVELER (BROWN)				
OA	1964	R: 5	STANDARD BOX $130	NO MATCHING BOTTLE MADE

357. front

			357. TREASURE CHEST ARTIST: ELMER LEHNHARDT	
AL	1961	R: 7	DOME BOX $375	MATCHING STEEL/GLASS BOTTLE $150

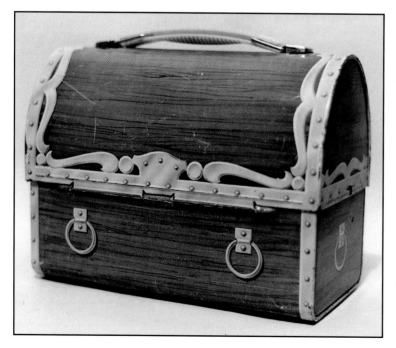

357. back

357. bottle

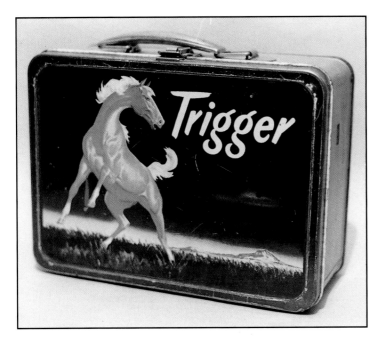

358. front

359. bottle

358. TRIGGER				
ROY ROGERS' FAMOUS HORSE; ARTIST: ED WEXLER; SAME FRONT & BACK				
AT	1956	R: 7	STANDARD BOX $220	NO MATCHING BOTTLE MADE

359. TROUT FLIES TALL STEEL/GLASS BOTTLE				
AT	1950s	R: 9	BOTTLE $50	SOLD SEPARATELY

360. front

360. bottle

360. UFO				
ARTIST: NICK LoBIANCO				
KST	1973	R: 5	STANDARD BOX $80	MATCHING SQUARE PLASTIC BOTTLE $30
				GENERIC SQUARE PLASTIC BOTTLE $10

361. front & bottle

362. bottle

361. UNDERDOG				
BASED ON THE TV SERIES; SAME FRONT & BACK				
OK	1974	R: 9	STANDARD BOX $1,500	MATCHING STEEL/GLASS BOTTLE $750

362. front

362. back

362. UNIVERSAL MOVIE MONSTERS				
ARTIST: ELMER LEHNHARDT				
AL	1979	R: 6	EMBOSSED STANDARD BOX $150	MATCHING ROUND PLASTIC BOTTLE $55

363. front & bottle

363. back & bottle

			363. U.S. MAIL	
			ARTIST: JIM BLACKBURN	
AL	1969	R: 5	DOME BOX $130	MATCHING ROUND PLASTIC BOTTLE $40

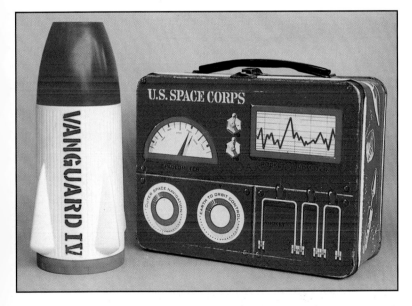

364. back

364. front & bottle

			364. U.S. SPACE CORPS	
			A RARE BOX, MADE RARER STILL BY THE ART ON THE BACK PRINTED UPSIDE DOWN; VANGUARD IV WAS A U.S. SATELLITE	
UN	1961	R: 9	STANDARD BOX PRINTED UPSIDE DOWN $500	VANGUARD IV MATCHING ROUND PLASTIC BOTTLE $150
		R: 7	STANDARD BOX PRINTED RIGHT SIDE UP $325	

365. front

365. back

365. "V" BASED ON THE TV SERIES				
AL	1984	R: 6	STANDARD BOX $150	MATCHING ROUND PLASTIC BOTTLE (NOT PICTURED) $50

366. front & bottle

366. V.W. BUS BELIEVED TO HAVE BEEN A PREMIUM FOR EITHER TEST DRIVING OR BUYING A BUS				
OG	1960s	R: 9	DOME BOX $1,000	GENERIC STYRO BOTTLE w/V.W. LOGO EMBOSSED ON TOP OF PLASTIC CUP $500

367. front & bottle

367. back

367. VOYAGE TO THE BOTTOM OF THE SEA				
BASED ON THE TV SERIES; ARTIST: ELMER LEHNHARDT				
AL	1967	R: 8	STANDARD BOX $475	MATCHING STEEL/GLASS BOTTLE $175

368. front

368. back

368. bottle

368. WAGS 'N WHISKERS				
KST	1978	R: 3	STANDARD BOX $45	MATCHING SQUARE PLASTIC BOTTLE $15

369. front

369. back

369. THE WALTONS				
BASED ON THE TV SERIES; ARTIST: ELMER LEHNHARDT				
AL	1974 – 1975	R: 4	EMBOSSED STANDARD BOX $75	MATCHING ROUND PLASTIC BOTTLE $35

369. bottle

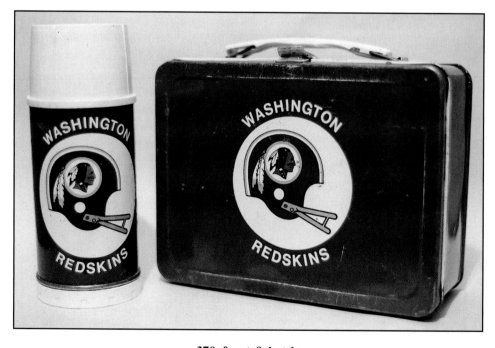

370. front & bottle

370. WASHINGTON REDSKINS				
SAME FRONT & BACK				
OK	1970	R: 8	STANDARD BOX $265	MATCHING STEEL/GLASS BOTTLE $160

371. front

372. bottle

371. WEAVE				
			SAME FRONT & BACK	
OA	1972	R: 4	STANDARD BOX $65	NO MATCHING BOTTLE MADE

372. front

372. back

372. WELCOME BACK, KOTTER				
			BASED ON THE TV SERIES STARRING JOHN TRAVOLTA; ARTIST: ELMER LEHNHARDT	
AL	1977	R: 4	STANDARD BOX $75	MATCHING ROUND PLASTIC BOTTLE $30

373. front

373. back

373. WESTERN (GEAR AROUND BAND)				
KST	1963	R: 6	STANDARD BOX $160	WESTERN THEME STEEL/GLASS BOTTLE $75

373. bottle

374. bottle

374. WILD BILL HICKOCK				
BASED ON THE TV SERIES; THE FIRST BOX TO HAVE A "TOOLED LEATHER" BAND; ARTIST: BOB BURTON; SAME FRONT & BACK				
AL	1955	R: 6	STANDARD BOX $185	MATCHING STEEL/GLASS BOTTLE $110

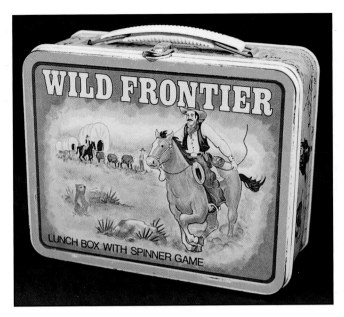

375. front

375. back

			375. WILD FRONTIER ARTIST: WILLIAM KULMAN	
OA	1977	R: 4	STANDARD BOX $70 CAME WITH OR WITHOUT SPINNER GAME	NO MATCHING BOTTLE MADE

376. front

376. bottle

			376. THE WILD WILD WEST ARTIST: ELMER LEHNHARDT	
AL	1969	R: 7	EMBOSSED STANDARD BOX $225	MATCHING ROUND PLASTIC BOTTLE $110

377. front & bottle

377. *WOODY WOODPECKER*				
ARTIST: ELMER LEHNHARDT				
AL	1972	R: 7	STANDARD BOX $250	MATCHING ROUND PLASTIC BOTTLE $75

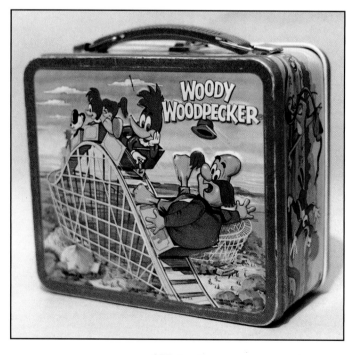

377. back

378.

378. *WORKMAN'S SLIDE-OUT*				
UNK	PAT. 1913	R: 6	DOME BOX $20	BOTTLE UNKNOWN

379.

380.

			379. WORKMAN'S BLUE BOX	
			PRECURSOR TO THE DECAL CHARACTER BOXES	
AL	1940s	R: 5	STANDARD BOX $25	BOTTLE UNKNOWN

| | | | 380. WORKMAN'S BLUE DOME BOX | |
| AT | 1940s | R: 5 | DOME BOX $20 | BOTTLE UNKNOWN |

381.

| | | | 381. WORKMAN'S GALVANIZED METAL BOX | |
| UNK | 1920s – 1930s | R: 6 | CARRY-ALL BOX $35 | CAME WITH PIE TRAY; NO BOTTLE MADE |

382. front

382. WORKMAN'S OR CHILD'S RED FLAT LUNCH KIT				
UNK	1940s	R: 7	BOX $35	BOTTLE UNKNOWN

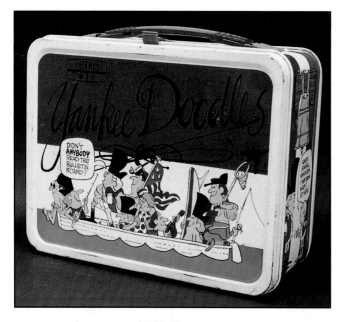

383. front

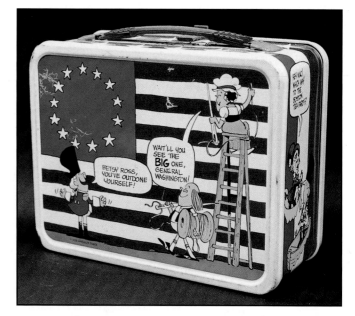

383. back

383. YANKEE DOODLES ATTRIBUTED TO ARTIST NICK LoBIANCO				
KST	1975	R: 3	STANDARD BOX $50	MATCHING SQUARE PLASTIC BOTTLE $20

384. front

384. YELLOW SUBMARINE				
BASED ON THE BEATLES MOVIE; ARTIST: NICK LoBIANCO				
KST	1968	R: 7	STANDARD BOX $500	MATCHING STEEL/GLASS BOTTLE $200

384. back

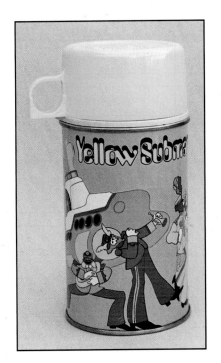

384. bottle

385. front

385. YOGI BEAR (BLACK RIM)				
BASED ON THE HANNA-BARBERA TV SERIES; ARTIST: ELMER LEHNHARDT				
AL	1961	R: 6	STANDARD BOX $200	MATCHING STEEL/GLASS BOTTLE $100

385. back

385. bottle

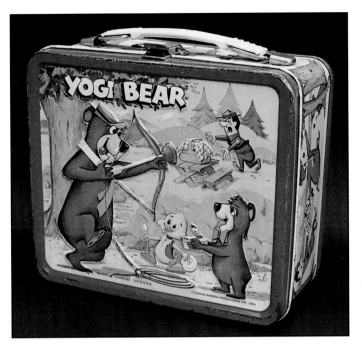

386. front

386. bottle

386. YOGI BEAR				
AL	1974	R: 5	STANDARD BOX $125	MATCHING ROUND PLASTIC BOTTLE $75

386. back

387. bottle

387. ZORRO (BLACK SKY)				
BOX FRONT IS ZORRO ON REARING HORSE WITH BLUE SKY; ARTISTS: BOB BURTON & ELMER LEHNHARDT				
AL	1958	R: 6	STANDARD BOX (NOT PICTURED) $175	STEEL/GLASS BOTTLE $130

ADAM-12: AL, 1973, R: 7, FLAT OR EMBOSSED BOX $100, MATCHING ROUND PLASTIC BOTTLE $50.

ALL AMERICAN RED BOX: w/MAP OF U.S.A. ON FACE, UN, 1954, R: 8, STANDARD BOX $375, TALL STEEL/GLASS UNIVERSAL VACUUM $100.

ANIMAL FRIENDS/YELLOW: SAME ART AS #8, BUT LETTERING IS YELLOW & SKY ONLY IS BLUE, OA, 1978, R: 3, STANDARD BOX $45, NO BOTTLE MADE.

BASKETWEAVE: DENSE BLUE CHECK PATTERN WITH SCROLLED CARTOUCHE IN CENTER OA, 1968, R: 4, STANDARD BOX $65, NO BOTTLE MADE.

BONANZA (BLACK): FRONT IS PA, JOE & HOSS ON HORSEBACK w/YELLOW SKY, AL, 1968, R: 6, STANDARD BOX $170, MATCHING STEEL/GLASS BOTTLE $120.

BOND XX: BOX IS SAME AS #38, BUT WITHOUT "SECRET AGENT" WORDING, OA, 1967, R: 7, STANDARD BOX $200, NO BOTTLE MADE.

BOSTON BRUINS: OK, 1974, R: 8, STANDARD BOX $475, MATCHING STEEL/GLASS BOTTLE $200.

CAMPBELL KIDS: FRONT & BACK ARE KIDS PLAYING: AT, 1959, R: 7, STANDARD BOX $200, PLASTIC BOTTLE w/ TOMATO SOUP, SIMILAR TO #42 BUT THINNER, $120.

CHAVO: BASED ON A MEXICAN TV SERIES, AL, 1979, R: 6, FLAT STANDARD BOX $140, EMB. STANDARD BOX $75, MATCHING ROUND PLASTIC BOTTLE $50.

CHILDREN (a.k.a. HAPPY CHILDREN): BLUE, OK, 1974, R: 6, STANDARD BOX $165, BLUE & WHITE PLASTIC BOTTLE $35.

CHILDREN (a.k.a. HAPPY CHILDREN): YELLOW, OK, 1974, R: 7, STANDARD BOX $230, YELLOW & WHITE PLASTIC BOTTLE $35.

COLOR ME HAPPY: OA, 1984, R: 5, STANDARD BOX $120, NO BOTTLE MADE.

THE CYCLIST: AL, 1979 – 1980, R: 4, EMBOSSED STANDARD BOX $65, MATCHING ROUND PLASTIC BOTTLE $35.

DANIEL BOONE: FRONT & BACK ARE BOONE CLUBBING INDIANS w/RIFLE, AL, 1955, R: 8, STANDARD BOX $375, MATCHING STEEL/GLASS BOTTLE $125.

DANIEL BOONE: FRONT BOONE CLUBBING INDIANS; BACK BOONE FIGHTING A BEAR, AL, 1965, R: 6, STANDARD BOX $180, MATCHING STEEL/GLASS BOTTLE $125.

WALT DISNEY WORLD/BLUE RIM "HAPPY 50 YEARS": AL, 1976, R: 5, EMBOSSED STANDARD BOX $110, MATCHING ROUND PLASTIC BOTTLE $25.

WALT DISNEY WORLD/WHITE RIM: AL, 1976, R: 6, STANDARD BOX $140, MATCHING ROUND PLASTIC BOTTLE $25.

DISNEYLAND CASTLE FRONT/BOAT BACK: AL, 1957, R: 6, STANDARD BOX $175, MATCHING STEEL/GLASS BOTTLE w/RIVERBOAT $120.

DISNEYLAND MONORAIL FRONT/SUBMARINE BACK: AL, 1960, R: 6, STANDARD BOX $200, MATCHING STEEL/GLASS BOTTLE w/CASTLE $120.

DR. SEUSS: AL, 1970 – 1971, R: 6, EMBOSSED STANDARD BOX $165, MATCHING ROUND PLASTIC BOTTLE $75.

FAT ALBERT: KST, 1973 – 1974, R: 3, STANDARD BOX $75, MATCHING STEEL/GLASS BOTTLE $25.

FLAG: NIGHT & DAY VIEWS OF WAVING AMERICAN FLAG, OA, 1973, R: 4, STANDARD BOX $70, NO BOTTLE MADE.

FLAG-O-RAMA: FRONT IS FLAGS OF U.N. MEMBER COUNTRIES, BACK IS PLAIN: UN, 1954, R: 8, STANDARD BOX $500, GENERIC STEEL/GLASS BOTTLE (SILVER w/RED "GEAR" CUP) $125.

FLINTSTONES (RED RIM): FRONT IS BEDROCK FESTIVAL; BACK IS MOONLIT SCENE, AL, 1971, R: 6, STANDARD BOX $160, MATCHING ROUND PLASTIC BOTTLE $70.

FRONTIER DAYS: OA, 1962 – 1964, R: 7, STANDARD BOX $220, NO BOTTLE MADE.

FROST FLOWERS: ALL-OVER PATTERN OF FLOWERS & SNOWFLAKES; CAME WITH MATCHING BAND & BOW BAND, OA, 1962 – 1964, R: 4, MATCHING BAND STANDARD BOX $70, BOW BAND STANDARD BOX $75, NO BOTTLE MADE.

FUNTASTIC WORLD OF HANNA-BARBERA: FRONT & BACK ARE SAME ANIMALS IN OLD CAR, KST, 1971, R: 5, STANDARD BOX $85, MATCHING SQUARE PLASTIC BOTTLE $30.

GI JOE: FRONT IS BATTLE SCENE; BACK IS TANK, KST, 1982, R: 3, STANDARD BOX $50, MATCHING SQUARE PLASTIC BOTTLE $20.

GHOSTLAND: CAME WITH & WITHOUT A SPINNER GAME ON THE BACK, OA, 1977, R: 3, STANDARD BOX $50, NO BOTTLE MADE.

GUNSMOKE DOUBLE "LL": FRONT IS MATT STANDING w/GUN POINTED; BACK IS STREET SHOOT-OUT; "MARSHAL" MISSPELLED "MARSHALL", AL, 1959, R: 9, STANDARD BOX $650, MATCHING STEEL/GLASS BOTTLE $115.

GUNSMOKE: SAME AS ABOVE BUT "MARSHAL" IS SPELLED CORRECTLY, AL, 1959, R: 6, STANDARD BOX $200, MATCHING STEEL/GLASS BOTTLE $115.

GUNSMOKE: FRONT IS MATT ON HORSEBACK w/GUN POINTING UP; BACK IS MISS KITTY, AL, 1972, R: 5, STANDARD BOX $130, MATCHING ROUND PLASTIC BOTTLE $75.

HOLLY HOBBIE (FLOWERS): FRONT IS TWO GIRLS FACING; BACK IS GIRLS AT WINDOW BOX, AL, 1982 – 1983, R: 3, EMBOSSED STANDARD BOX $25, MATCHING ROUND PLASTIC BOTTLE $15.

JACK & JILL: OA, 1982, R: 7, STANDARD BOX $325, NO BOTTLE MADE.

JOE PALOOKA: CC, 1949, R: 7, CARRY-ALL BOX $140, NO BOTTLE MADE.

JOHNNY LIGHTNING: AL, 1970, R: 4, EMBOSSED STANDARD BOX $100, MATCHING ROUND PLASTIC BOTTLE $50.

JONATHAN LIVINGSTON SEAGULL: AL, 1974, R: 3, STANDARD BOX $55, MATCHING ROUND PLASTIC BOTTLE $30.

JUNIOR MISS: FRONT & BACK SHOW BRANCH w/ VARIOUS FLOWERS, AL, 1963 – 1964, R: 6, STANDARD BOX $160, MATCHING STEEL/GLASS BOTTLE $70.

KISS: KST, 1977, R: 5, STANDARD BOX $200, MATCHING SQUARE PLASTIC BOTTLE $75.

LANCE LINK: KST, 1971, R: 5, STANDARD BOX $125, MATCHING STEEL/GLASS BOTTLE $75.

LAUGH-IN (TRICYCLE): AL, 1968, R: 6, STANDARD BOX $150, BOTTLE SAME AS HELMET BOX $65.

LAWMAN: KST, 1961, R: 6, STANDARD BOX $200, BOTTLE SAME AS WESTERN BOX $75.

LITTLE FRIENDS: AL, 1982, R: 9, STANDARD BOX $700, MATCHING ROUND PLASTIC BOTTLE $250.

LONE RANGER (BLUE BAND): SAME AS #204 EXCEPT FOR BAND COLOR, AD, 1954, R: 9, STANDARD BOX $500, NO BOTTLE MADE.

LOST IN SPACE: KST, 1967, R: 7, DOME BOX $600, MATCHING ROUND PLASTIC BOTTLE $75.

MICKEY MOUSE OVAL w/TWO WIRE HANDLES: GPF, 1935 – 1937, R: 9, CARRY-ALL BOX $1,500, CONTAINED PIE TRAY , NO BOTTLE MADE.

MOD FLORAL: ALL-OVER STYLIZED PATTERN OF OUTLINED BRIGHT FLOWERS, OK, 1975 – 1978, R: 7, STANDARD BOX $260, MATCHING STEEL/GLASS BOTTLE $150.

MUPPETS/ANIMAL: KST, 1979, R: 3, STANDARD BOX $45, MATCHING ROUND PLASTIC BOTTLE $15.

NHL: OK, 1970, R: 8, STANDARD BOX $500, MATCHING STEEL/GLASS BOTTLE $200.

OUR FRIENDS: OK/UN, 1970, R: 9, STANDARD BOX $550, MATCHING STEEL/GLASS BOTTLE $200.

PARA-MEDIC: OA, 1978, R: 3, BOX WITH MEDICAL TOYS $50, NO BOTTLE MADE.

PEANUTS (RED RIM): KST, 1973, R: 3, STANDARD BOX $55, MATCHING SQUARE PLASTIC BOTTLE $15.

PEANUTS (RED BAND): KST, 1980, R: 3, STANDARD BOX $60, MATCHING OR GENERIC PLASTIC BOTTLE $20.

PELÉ: KST, 1975, R: 5, STANDARD BOX $85, MATCHING SQUARE PLASTIC BOTTLE $35.

PINK GINGHAM: ALL-OVER PINK & WHITE GINGHAM CHECKS w/WHITE RIM, KST, 1976, R: 3, STANDARD BOX $50, GENERIC PINK SQUARE PLASTIC BOTTLE $10.

PINOCCHIO: ROUND, LIDDED PAIL w/SINGLE HANDLE, LIB, 1938 – 1941, R: 5, PAIL $200, NO BOTTLE MADE.

PINOCCHIO: RECTANGULAR CARRY-ALL BOX w/TWO HANDLES, LIB, 1938 – 1941, R: 5, CARRY-ALL BOX $200, NO BOTTLE MADE.

PIT STOP: OA, 1968, R: 6, STANDARD BOX $250, GENERIC STEEL/GLASS BOTTLE $20.

PLAID: SINCE THERE ARE MORE THAN 19 KNOWN DIFFERENT PLAID BOXES AND BOTTLES WITH DESCRIPTIONS SOUNDING VERY MUCH ALIKE, OUR PLAID PROBE IS LIMITED TO ONLY THE ONES PICTURED.

POLICE PATROL: AL, 1978, R: 7, STANDARD BOX $200, MATCHING STEEL/GLASS BOTTLE $75.

ROBIN HOOD: DISNEY CARTOON CHARACTERS, AL, 1974, R: 4, STANDARD BOX $100, MATCHING ROUND PLASTIC BOTTLE $40.

ROY ROGERS: NARROW, SAME FRONT AS #296 BUT BACK HAS ONLY ONE BRAND AND BAND IS WOOD GRAIN, AT, 1954, R: 7, STANDARD BOX $200, SAME BOTTLE AS #296.

ROY ROGERS: RED BAND, SAME FRONT & BACK AS #296, BUT BAND IS RED, AT, 1954, R: 8, STANDARD BOX $250, SAME BOTTLE AS #296.

ROY ROGERS: LEATHER HANDLE, SAME FRONT & BACK AS #296 w/BRANDS ADDED INSIDE LARIAT, AND HANDLE IS LEATHER STRAP, AT, 1954, R: 8, STANDARD BOX $275, MATCHING STEEL/GLASS BOTTLE $200, (TWO VERSIONS: FIGURAL OF ROY, DALE, TRIGGER & BULLET SAME AS 296, AND ALL-OVER WOOD GRAIN WITH BRANDS.

ROY ROGERS: RED BAND SAME FRONT & BACK AS #297, BUT BAND IS RED, AT, 1955, R: 7, STANDARD BOX $150, SAME BOTTLE AS #296.

ROY ROGERS: COWHIDE BLUE BAND, FRONT SAME AS BACK OF #297 w/EIGHT SCENES; BACK IS COWHIDE w/BRANDS, AT, 1955, R: 7, STANDARD BOX $180, SAME BOTTLE AS #297.

ROY ROGERS (ON RAIL/RED BAND): SAME FRONT & BACK AS #298, BUT BAND IS RED, AT, 1957, STANDARD BOX $180, BOTTLE SAME AS #297 BUT WITH YELLOW SKY $165.

ROY ROGERS CHOW WAGON: AT, 1955, R: 7, DOME BOX $300, SAME BOTTLE AS #297 BUT WITH YELLOW SKY.

SCHOOL DAYS: MICKEY MOUSE & DONALD DUCK, AL, 1984, R: 8, STANDARD BOX $400, MATCHING ROUND PLASTIC BOTTLE $150.

SLEEPING BEAUTY (BLUE RIM): RARE BOX FROM CANADA; FRONT IS BEAUTY & PRINCE FACING OVER TREE; BACK IS BEAUTY & OWL, GSW, 1972, R: 9, STANDARD BOX $500, BOTTLE UNKNOWN.

SMOKEY BEAR: OK, 1975 – 1978, R: 8, STANDARD BOX $375, MATCHING ROUND PLASTIC BOTTLE $175.

SNOW WHITE: LIB, 1938 – 1941, R: 9, CARRY-ALL BOX $250, NO BOTTLE MADE.

SPEED BUGGY: KST, 1974, R: 4, STANDARD BOX $70, MATCHING SQUARE PLASTIC BOTTLE $25.

STRAWBERRYLAND: AL, 1981, R: 3, STANDARD BOX $30, MATCHING ROUND PLASTIC BOTTLE $15.

SUPER HEROES: AL, 1976, R: 4, STANDARD BOX $80, MATCHING ROUND PLASTIC BOTTLE $30.

TAPESTRY: ALL-OVER PINK & BLUE FLORAL PATTERN ON WHITE BOX, OA, 1966, R: 5, STANDARD BOX $45, NO BOTTLE MADE.

TOPPIE: PROMOTIONAL ITEM DISTRIBUTED ONLY IN OHIO, AT, 1957, R: 10, STANDARD BOX $2,500, MATCHING STEEL/GLASS BOTTLE $1,000.

240 ROBERT: AL, 1978, R 10+, STANDARD BOX $4,000, BOTTLE UNKNOWN.

UPBEAT: RED DOME BOX WITH ONE WHITE FLOWER ON ALL FOUR SIDES, SEARS, 1975, R: 8, DOME BOX $85, CAME WITH ELECTRIC HAIR CURLERS INSIDE.

WAGON TRAIN: KST, 1964, R: 7, STANDARD BOX $200, SAME BOTTLE AS WESTERN GEAR BAND BOX #373.

WESTERN (PLAIN TAN BAND): SAME AS #373 BUT w/PLAIN BAND, KST, 1964, R: 8, STANDARD BOX $350, SAME BOTTLE AS WESTERN GEAR BAND BOX.

WINNIE THE POOH: KST, 1964, R: 8, EMBOSSED OR FLAT STANDARD BOX $250, MATCHING STEEL/GLASS BOTTLE $75.

WOODY WOODPECKER: RED DOME BOX w/SMALL WOODY IN A CIRCLE OF STARS, UNK, R: 10, DOME BOX $900, BOTTLE UNKNOWN.

ZORRO RED SKY: FRONT SAME AS BLACK SKY BOX, BUT SKY IS RED, AL, 1966, R: 7, STANDARD BOX $200, MATCHING STEEL/GLASS BOTTLE $150.

Wags 'n Whiskers, shown on page 225.

Western (gear around band), shown on page 228.

388. front & bottle

			388. ALICE IN WONDERLAND	
AL	1974	R: 6	STANDARD BOX $225	MATCHING ROUND PLASTIC BOTTLE $55

389. front & bottle

			389. ALVIN ARTIST: NICK LoBIANCO	
BV	1963	R: 8	STANDARD BOX $450	MATCHING STEEL/GLASS BOTTLE $150

390. front & bottle

			390. ANNIE	
			ARTIST: BEVERLY BURGE	
AL	1981	R: 4	STANDARD BOX $80	MATCHING ROUND PLASTIC BOTTLE $30

391. front

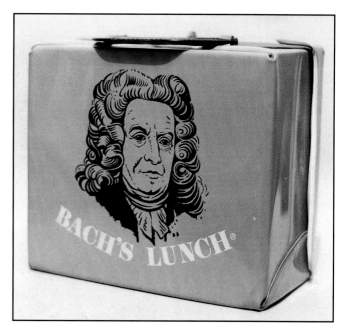

391. back

			391. BACH'S LUNCH (BLUE)	
			A VERSION WAS ALSO MADE IN RED; SAME VALUE	
VBI	1975	R: 6	STANDARD BOX $150	STYRO BOTTLE $10

392. front

394. front

			392. BALLERINA ON LILY PAD	
AR	1960s	R: 7	STANDARD BOX $75	BOTTLE UNKNOWN

			393. THE BANANA SPLITS ARTIST: NICK LoBIANCO	
KST	1969	R: 6	STANDARD BOX $500	MATCHING STEEL/GLASS BOTTLE $150

393. front & bottle

			394. BARBARINO ARTIST: ELMER LEHNHARDT	
AL	1977	R: 7	BRUNCH BAG $300	MATCHING ROUND PLASTIC BOTTLE $40

395. front

395. bottle

395. BARBIE®				
ARTIST: NICK LoBIANCO				
KST	1962	R: 4	STANDARD BOX $450	MATCHING STEEL/GLASS BOTTLE $75

396. front

396. BARBIE® & FRANCIE™				
ARTIST: NICK LoBIANCO				
KST	1965	R: 5	STANDARD BOX $170	MATCHING STEEL/GLASS BOTTLE $75

397. front

397. bottle

397. BARBIE® & MIDGE® ARTIST: NICK LoBIANCO				
KST	1964 – 1965??	R: 6	STANDARD BOX $170	MATCHING STEEL/GLASS BOTTLE $75

398. front

398. BARBIE® & MIDGE® ARTIST: NICK LoBIANCO				
KST	1964	R: 7	DOME BOX $600	SAME BOTTLE AS BARBIE & MIDGE STANDARD BOX

243

399. front

399. bottle

399. WORLD OF BARBIE® (BLUE)				
KST	1971	R: 4	STANDARD BOX $100	MATCHING STEEL/GLASS BOTTLE $25

400. front

400. back

400. WORLD OF BARBIE® (PINK)				
KST	1977	R: 4	STANDARD BOX $100	MATCHING STEEL/GLASS BOTTLE $25

401. front

401. *BEANY & CECIL (WHITE)*				
KST	1962 – 1963	R: 8	STANDARD BOX $600	PLAIN HOLTEMP STEEL/GLASS BOTTLE $40

402. front

402. bottle

402. *BEANY & CECIL (BROWN)*				
KST	1963	R: 8	STANDARD BOX $600	MATCHING STEEL/GLASS BOTTLE $200

403. front

	**403. BULLWINKLE** ARTIST: CHARLIE BROWN
KST	1962	R: 8	STANDARD BOX $500	GENERIC STEEL/GLASS BOTTLE $50

404. front & bottle

	**404. CAPTAIN KANGAROO** ARTIST: NICK LoBIANCO
UNK	1964	R: 8	STANDARD BOX $525	MATCHING STEEL/GLASS BOTTLE $160

405. front & bottle

405. CAROUSEL				
AL	1962	R: 8	STANDARD BOX $475	MATCHING STEEL/GLASS BOTTLE $150

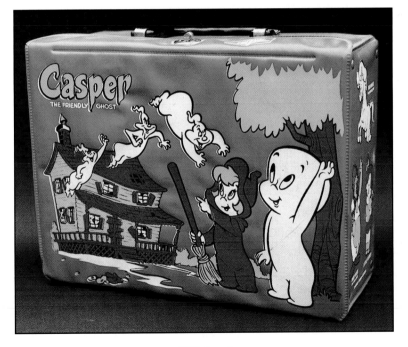

406. front

406. bottle

406. CASPER				
KST	1966	R: 8	STANDARD BOX $525	MATCHING STEEL/GLASS BOTTLE $150

407. front

408.

			407. COCO THE CLOWN	
GA	1970s	R: 5	STANDARD BOX $125	STYRO BOTTLE $10

			408. COMBO	
AL	1960s	R: 6	BRUNCH BAG $200	BOTTLE UNKNOWN

409. front

409. back

			409. COTTAGE	
KST	1974	R: 5	BOX $135	BOTTLE UNKNOWN

410. front

410. back

410. DENIM				
KST	1970s	R: 4	STANDARD BOX $100	MATCHING STEEL/GLASS BOTTLE $20

410. bottle

411. front

411. DEPUTY DAWG				
TH (KST)	1964	R: 8	STANDARD BOX $1,500	BOTTLE UNKNOWN

412. front

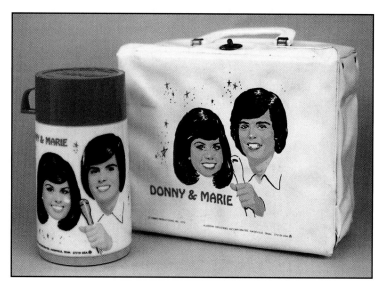

413. front & bottle

414. front

412. "DISNEY CHARACTERS"				
WALT DISNEY PROD	UNK	R: 7	LUNCH OR TOTE BAG $50	BOTTLE UNKNOWN

413. DONNY & MARIE (LONG HAIR)				
AL	1976 – 1977	R: 5	STANDARD BOX $125	MATCHING ROUND PLASTIC BOTTLE $35

414. DONNY & MARIE (LONG HAIR)				
AL	1976 – 1977	R: 5	BRUNCH BAG $150	MATCHING ROUND PLASTIC BOTTLE $35

415. front & bottle

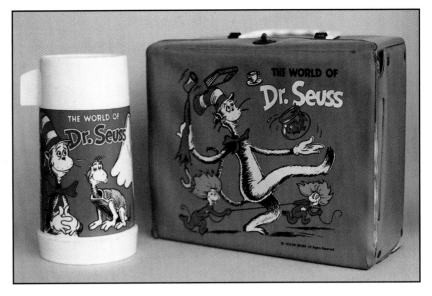

416. front & bottle

415. DOTS (a.k.a. SIXTEEN DOTS OR REGAL)				
AL	1968	R: 7	BRUNCH BAG $240	MATCHING STEEL/GLASS BOTTLE $75

416. DR. SEUSS ARTIST: THEODORE GEISEL (DR. SEUSS)				
AL	1970	R: 8	STANDARD BOX $600	MATCHING ROUND PLASTIC BOTTLE $75

Photo by Fred Carlson

417. front & bottle

Photo by Fred Carlson

417. bottom of bottle

417. DRAWSTRING BAG				
UN	1950s	R: 9	DRAWSTRING BAG $85	MATCHING STEEL/GLASS BOTTLE $30

251

418. front

419. front & bottle

418. EAT				
CURRENT, INC. TAIWAN	1986	R: 6	BAG $25	BOTTLE UNKNOWN

419. FAMILIES ABOVE THE BEST				
UNK BUT PROBABLY DART	UNK	R: 7	STANDARD BOX $240	STYRO BOTTLE $10

420. front

420. FESS PARKER AS DANIEL BOONE BASED ON THE TV SERIES				
SPP	1960s	R: 8	STANDARD BOX $500	NO BOTTLE MADE

421. front

421. bottle

421. FROG FLAUTIST				
AL	1975	R: 4	STANDARD BOX $125	MATCHING ROUND PLASTIC BOTTLE $30

422. front & bottle

422. FUNNY FISH				
AL	1975	R: 7	BRUNCH BAG $225	MATCHING ROUND PLASTIC BOTTLE $60

423. front & bottle

423. GIGI				
SAME BLACK POODLE AS SUZETTE BRUNCH BAG; BASED ON A DOG BELONGING TO AN ALADDIN EXECUTIVE				
AL	1962	R: 7	STANDARD BOX $250	MATCHING STEEL/GLASS BOTTLE $80

424. front & bottle

425. front & bottle

424. GO GO				
AL	1966	R: 7	STANDARD BOX $250	MATCHING STEEL/GLASS BOTTLE $75

425. GO GO				
AL	1966	R: 8	BRUNCH BAG $310	MATCHING STEEL/GLASS BOTTLE $75

426. front & bottle

426. HARLEQUIN				
AL	1962	R: 7	BRUNCH BAG $250	MATCHING STEEL/GLASS BOTTLE $75

427. HOLLY HOBBIE ARTIST: BEVERLY BURGE				
AL	1972	R: 4	STANDARD BOX $110	MATCHING ROUND PLASTIC BOTTLE $30

427. front

428. front

428. HOLLY HOBBIE ARTIST: ANN CUMMINGS				
AL	1978	R: 6	BRUNCH BAG $160	MATCHING ROUND PLASTIC BOTTLE $30

255

429. front

430. front & bottle

			429. I LOVE A PARADE	
BV	1970	R: 6	STANDARD BOX $55	STYRO BOTTLE $10

			430. ICE CREAM w/PINK GINGHAM BACKGROUND	
AL	1975	R: 4	STANDARD BOX $110	MATCHING ROUND PLASTIC BOTTLE $25

431. front & bottle

			431. IT'S A SMALL WORLD	
AL	1968	R: 8	STANDARD BOX $325	MATCHING STEEL/GLASS BOTTLE $120

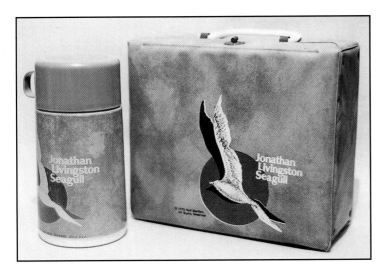

432. front & bottle

434. front

432. *JONATHAN LIVINGSTON SEAGULL*				
ARTIST: JOHN HENRY				
AL	1973	R: 6	STANDARD BOX $170	MATCHING ROUND PLASTIC BOTTLE $35

433. *JUNIOR NURSE*				
ARTISTS: CHARLIE BROWN & NICK LoBIANCO				
KST	1963	R: 8	STANDARD BOX $385	MATCHING STEEL/GLASS BOTTLE $110

433. front & bottle

434. *KABOODLE KIT (WHITE)*				
ALSO CAME IN PINK; SAME VALUE				
AL	1960s	R: 6	STANDARD BOX $185	BOTTLE UNKNOWN

435. front & bottle

			435. KEWTIE PIE	
AL	1967	R: 5	STANDARD BOX $140	MATCHING STEEL/GLASS BOTTLE $80

436. front

437. front

			436. L'IL JODIE	
BA	1985	R: 4	PUFFY BAG $110	BOTTLE UNKNOWN

			437. LITTLE OLD SCHOOLHOUSE	
DA	1974	R: 4	BOX $100	BOTTLE UNKNOWN

438. front

438. LUNCH 'n MUNCH				
AT	1959	R: 9	STANDARD BOX $700	BOTTLE SAME AS ASTRONAUT DOME #13 & SATELLITE #300

439. front & bottle

440. front & bottle

439. MAM'ZELLE ARTIST: SALLY AUGUSTINI				
AL	1970 – 1971	R: 7	STANDARD BOX $200	MATCHING ROUND PLASTIC BOTTLE $85

440. MARY POPPINS				
AL	1973	R: 5	STANDARD BOX $160	MATCHING ROUND PLASTIC BOTTLE $75

441. front

442. front

			441. MICKEY MOUSE KABOODLE KIT	
UNK	1963	R: 8	STANDARD BOX $365	BOTTLE UNKNOWN

			442. MOD MISS (BLUE)	
AL	1970	R: 4	BRUNCH BAG $120	BOTTLE UNKNOWN

443. front, bottle & wallet

			443. MUSHROOMS	
AL	1973	R: 5	STANDARD BOX w/WALLET $160	MATCHING ROUND PLASTIC BOTTLE $50

444. front & bottle

		444. MUSHROOMS		
AL	1973	R: 5	BRUNCH BAG $160	MATCHING ROUND PLASTIC BOTTLE $50

445. front & bottle

		445. OWLS		
AL	1970s	R: 4	BRUNCH BAG $110	MATCHING ROUND PLASTIC BOTTLE $60

446. front

446. PEANUTS (RED) ARTIST: NICK LoBIANCO				
KST	1967 – 1968	R: 4	STANDARD BOX $125	MATCHING STEEL/GLASS BOTTLE $35

446. back

446. bottle

447. front & bottle

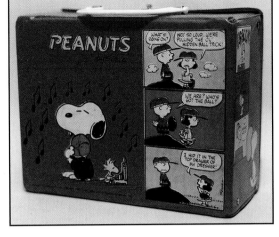

447. back

447. *PEANUTS (RED w/MUSICAL NOTES)* ARTIST: NICK LoBIANCO				
KST	1967	R: 5	STANDARD BOX $125	MATCHING SQUARE PLASTIC BOTTLE $20

448. front

448. back

448. *PEANUTS (GREEN)* ARTIST: NICK LoBIANCO				
KST	1971 – 1972	R: 5	STANDARD BOX $165	SAME BOTTLE AS #446

449. front & bottle

449. back

449. PEANUTS (WHITE) ARTIST: NICK LoBIANCO				
KST	1973	R: 4	STANDARD BOX $130	MATCHING SQUARE PLASTIC BOTTLE OR SAME STEEL/GLASS BOTTLE AS #446 $20

450. front & bottle

450. PEANUTS ARTIST: NICK LoBIANCO				
KST	1977	R: 5	MUNCHIES BAG $175	MATCHING SQUARE PLASTIC BOTTLE $45

451. front

451. bottle

451. PEBBLES & BAMM BAMM				
ARTIST: NICK LoBIANCO				
GA	1978	R: 7	STANDARD BOX $280	MATCHING ROUND PLASTIC BOTTLE $85

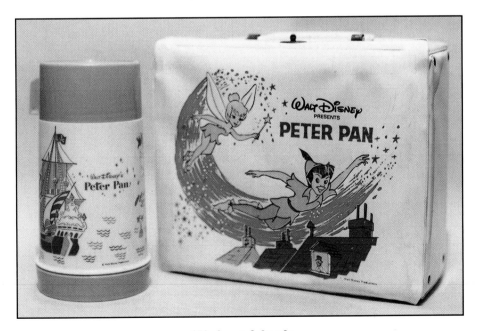

452. front & bottle

452. PETER PAN				
AL	1969	R: 7	STANDARD BOX $225	MATCHING ROUND PLASTIC BOTTLE $85

453. front & bottle

			453. PINK PANTHER	
AL	1980	R: 4	STANDARD BOX $125	MATCHING ROUND PLASTIC BOTTLE $45

			454. PONYTAIL EATS 'N TREATS (BLUE) ALSO CAME IN PINK OR RED	
AT	1959	R: 7	STANDARD BOX $225	CORSAGE STEEL/GLASS BOTTLE LIKE #70 BUT w/RED CUP $45

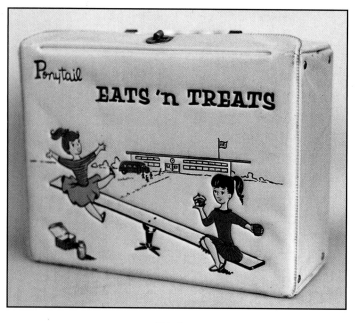

454. front

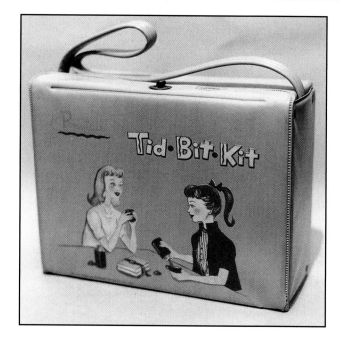

455. front

			455. PONYTAIL TID-BIT-KIT (BLUE)	
KST	1962	R: 7	STANDARD BOX $225	CORSAGE STEEL/GLASS BOTTLE LIKE #70 BUT w/RED CUP $45

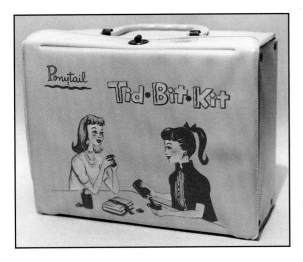

456. front

457. front

456. PONYTAIL TID-BIT-KIT (PINK)

TH	1960s	R: 7	STANDARD BOX $190	CORSAGE STEEL/GLASS BOTTLE LIKE #70 BUT w/RED CUP $55

457. POPEYE

HECHO EN MEXICO MOD 900 ZUMY	1981	R: 8	BOX $200	BOTTLE UNKNOWN

457. back

458. front & bottle

458. PRINCESS

AL	1963	R: 8	STANDARD BOX $200	MATCHING STEEL/GLASS BOTTLE $95

459. front & bottle

460. front

			459. PSYCHEDELIC BLUE	
KST	1970	R: 6	SHORT MUNCHIES BAG $200	MATCHING STEEL/GLASS BOTTLE $65

			460. PSYCHEDELIC YELLOW	
AL	1969	R: 7	STANDARD BOX $240	BOTTLE SAME AS PSYCHEDELIC METAL DOME BOX #278

461. front & bottle

			461. THE PUSSYCATS	
AL	1968	R: 7	STANDARD BOX $225	MATCHING STEEL/GLASS BOTTLE $85

462. front

463. front & bottle

462. "QUILTED SQUARES"				
UNK	UNK	R: 7	STANDARD BOX $125	BOTTLE UNKNOWN

463. RAGGEDY ANN & ANDY ARTIST: ANN CUMMINGS				
AL	1973	R: 5	BRUNCH BAG $165	MATCHING ROUND PLASTIC BOTTLE $45

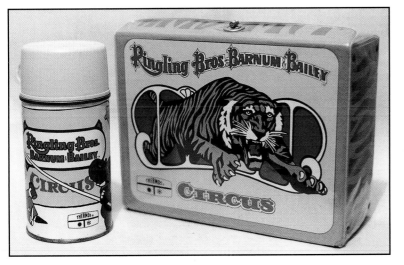

464. front & bottle

464. back

464. RINGLING BROS. BARNUM & BAILEY CIRCUS				
KST	1970	R: 8	STANDARD BOX $450	MATCHING STEEL/GLASS BOTTLE $125

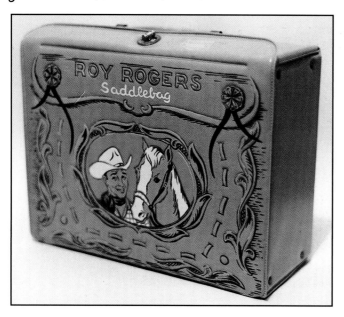

465. front

467. front

465. ROY ROGERS SADDLE BAG (BROWN)				
KST	1960	R: 7	STANDARD BOX $260	SAME BOTTLE AS #297 BUT WITH YELLOW SKY

466. SABRINA BASED ON THE TV CARTOON SERIES; ARTIST: DEE WENNER				
AL	1972	R: 7	STANDARD BOX $240	MATCHING ROUND PLASTIC BOTTLE $70

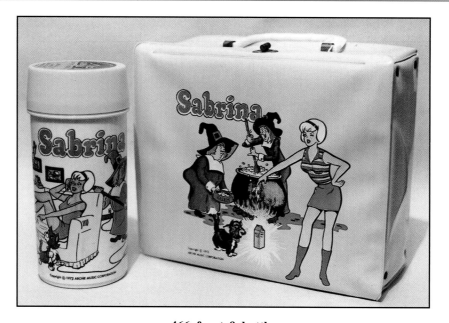

466. front & bottle

467. SCHOOL BUS				
UNK	1985	R: 4	PUFFY $120	BOTTLE UNKNOWN

468. front

468. *"SCHOOL NAME"*				
UNK	UNK	R: 9	STANDARD BOX $200	BOTTLE UNKNOWN

469. front & bottle

470. front & bottle

469. *SESAME STREET (ORANGE)* ARTIST: BEVERLY BURGE				
AL	1979	R: 4	STANDARD BOX $110	MATCHING ROUND PLASTIC BOTTLE $25

470. *SESAME STREET (YELLOW)* ARTIST: BEVERLY BURGE				
AL	1981	R: 4	STANDARD BOX $100	MATCHING ROUND PLASTIC BOTTLE $25

471. front & back

471. SHARI LEWIS ARTIST: ELMER LEHNHARDT				
AL	1963	R: 8	STANDARD BOX $480	MATCHING STEEL/GLASS BOTTLE $135

472. front & bottle

473. front

472. SIZZLERS				
KST	1971	R: 6	STANDARD BOX $220	MATCHING STEEL/GLASS BOTTLE $75

473. SKIPPER ARTIST: NICK LoBIANCO				
KST	1965	R: 7	STANDARD BOX $250	MATCHING STEEL/GLASS BOTTLE $95

474. front & bottle

476. front & bottle

474. SLEEPING BEAUTY				
AL	1970	R: 7	STANDARD BOX $250	MATCHING ROUND PLASTIC BOTTLE $85

475. SMOKEY "THE BEAR"				
KST	1965 – 1966	R: 8	STANDARD BOX $500	MATCHING STEEL/GLASS BOTTLE $150

475. front & bottle

476. SOPHISTICATE ("ROSE NEEDLEPOINT")				
AL	1972	R: 4	BRUNCH BAG $120	MATCHING ROUND PLASTIC BOTTLE $55

477. front & bottle

478. front & bottle

			477. SOPHISTICATE ("ROSE TAPESTRY")	
AL	1970s	R: 4	BRUNCH BAG $135	MATCHING STEEL/GLASS BOTTLE $60

			478. SOPHISTICATE ("SNAKESKIN")	
AL	1969	R: 5	BRUNCH BAG $170	MATCHING ROUND PLASTIC BOTTLE $70

479. front & bottle

			479. SOPHISTICATE ("TAPESTRY")	
AL	1970	R: 4	BRUNCH BAG $135	MATCHING ROUND PLASTIC BOTTLE $55

480. front & bottle

482. front & bottle

480. STARS & STRIPES				
KST	1970	R: 5	MUNCHIES BAG $180	MATCHING STEEL/GLASS BOTTLE $70

481. THE STEWARDESS ARTIST: JOHN HENRY				
AL	1962	R: 9	STANDARD BOX $700	MATCHING STEEL/GLASS BOTTLE $160

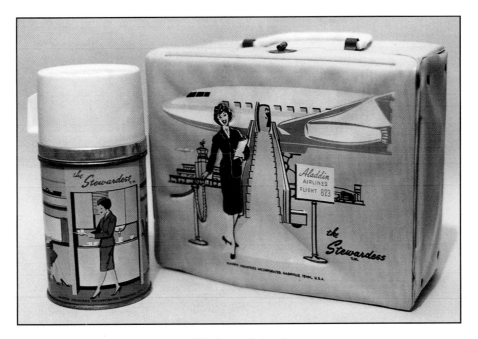

481. front & bottle

482. STRAWBERRY SHORTCAKE				
AL	1980	R: 4	STANDARD BOX $125	MATCHING PLASTIC BOTTLE $25

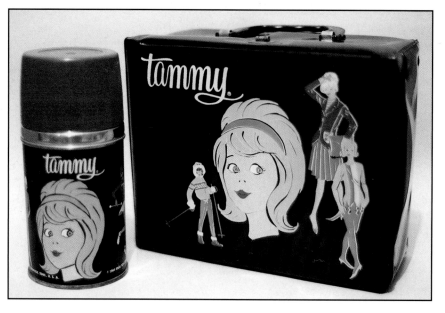

484. front & bottle

483. SUZETTE				
SAME BLACK POODLE AS GIGI BOX; BASED ON A DOG BELONGING TO AN ALADDIN EXECUTIVE				
AL	1970 – 1971	R: 7	BRUNCH BAG $260	MATCHING PLASTIC BOTTLE $85

484. TAMMY				
AL	1964 – 1965	R: 7	STANDARD BOX $270	MATCHING STEEL/GLASS BOTTLE $110

483. front

485. front

485. TAMMY & PEPPER				
AL	1965 – 1967	R: 7	STANDARD BOX $260	MATCHING STEEL/GLASS BOTTLE $110

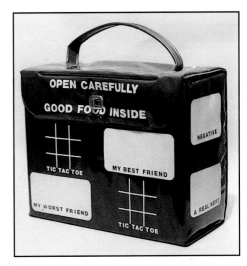

487. front

486. front

			486. TENNESSEE TUXEDO	
			SAME BOX SOLD WITH BULLWINKLE, DUDLEY DO-RIGHT, TENNESSEE TUXEDO OR UNDERDOG PAPER PANELS	
AR	1970s	R: 10	STANDARD BOX $2,500	STYRO BOTTLE $10

			487. TIC TAC TOE (BLUE OR RED)	
BA	UNK	R: 4	STANDARD BOX $110	BOTTLE UNKNOWN

488. front

			488. TINKER BELL	
AL	1968	R: 7	STANDARD BOX $275	MATCHING ROUND PLASTIC BOTTLE $95

489. front & bottle

490. front

489. TWIGGY				
ARTIST: ELMER LEHNHARDT				
AL	1967	R: 7	STANDARD BOX $285	MATCHING STEEL/GLASS BOTTLE $125

490. UNDERDOG				
AR	1972	R: 10	STANDARD BOX $2,000	STYRO BOTTLE $20

491. front & bottle

491. WONDER WOMAN (BLUE)				
ARTIST: BOB JONES				
AL	1977	R: 6	STANDARD BOX $175	MATCHING ROUND PLASTIC BOTTLE $45

493. back

493. front

493. YOSEMITE SAM ARTIST: NICK LoBIANCO				
KST	1971	R: 8	STANDARD BOX $500	MATCHING STEEL/GLASS BOTTLE $125

494. front & bottle

493. bottle

494. ZIGGY'S MUNCH BOX ARTIST: BEVERLY BURGE				
AL	1979	R: 5	STANDARD BOX $150	MATCHING ROUND PLASTIC BOTTLE $35

AIRLINE STEWARDESS: AR, 1972, R: 7, STANDARD BOX $150, STYROFOAM BOTTLE $10.

AIRPORT: AR, 1972, R: 7, STANDARD BOX $150, STYRO FOAM BOTTLE $10.

ALL AMERICAN: BV, 1976, R: 7, STANDARD BOX $125, STYROFOAM BOTTLE $10.

ALL DRESSED UP: BV, 1970s, R: 7, STANDARD BOX $125, STYROFOAM BOTTLE $10.

APPLE: UNK, 87, R: 7, CUBE $35, MATCHING PLASTIC BOTTLE $20.

BACKGAMMON: KST, 1960s, R: 6, MUNCHIES BAG $160, HOLTEMP BOTTLE $45.

BALLET: UN, 1961, R: 8, STANDARD BOX $750, BOTTLE UNKNOWN.

BALLERINA: AL, 1962, R: 7, STANDARD BOX $275, MATCHING STEEL/GLASS BOTTLE $110.

BALLERINA (TWO GIRLS): AR, 1960s, R: 8, STANDARD BOX $125, BOTTLE UNKNOWN.

BAND AID: UNK, 1980s, R: 7, BRUNCH BAG $155, BOTTLE UNKNOWN.

BARBIE & MIDGE: KST, 1965, R: 6, STANDARD BOX $270, MATCHING STEEL/GLASS BOTTLE $110.

BARBIE & MIDGE w/S.V. HANDLE: KST, 1964, R: 7, STANDARD BOX $270, MATCHING STEEL/GLASS BOTTLE $110.

BARBIE & MIDGE: KST, 1963, R: 6, MUNCHIES BAG, $150.

BARBIE: KST, 1988, R: 6, SOFTY $75, PLASTIC BOTTLE $20.

BARBIE LUNCHBOX PONYTAIL: KST, 1961, R: 8, (OVERSIZE) BOX $800. MATCHING STEEL/GLASS BOTTLE $110.

BARN: UNK, UNK, R: 7, DOME BOX $120, BOTTLE UNKNOWN.

BARN: DA, 1979, R: 7, PUFFY $100, BOTTLE UNKNOWN.

BARNUM'S ANIMALS: AD, 1978, R: 7, STANDARD BOX $75, BOTTLE UNKNOWN.

BATMAN: KST, 1991, R: 7, SOFTY $75, MATCHING PLASTIC BOTTLE $25.

BEATLES (SEVERAL COLORS): AIR, 1965 – 1966, R: 8, STANDARD BOX $1,000, NO BOTTLE MADE.

BEATLES: AL, 1966, R: 9, BRUNCH BAG $600, MATCHING STEEL/GLASS BOTTLE $600.

BEATLES KABOODLE KIT: SPP, 1965 – 1966, CAME IN WHITE, YELLOW, LAVENDER OR BLUE, STANDARD BOX $500, NO MATCHING BOTTLE MADE.

BETSY CLARK: KST, 1977, R: 6, STANDARD BOX $155, MATCHING PLASTIC BOTTLE $15.

BLACK (PLAIN SOLID COLOR): AL, 1970, R: 8, STANDARD BOX $55, BOTTLE UNKNOWN.

BLACK (PLAIN SOLID COLOR): UNK, UNK, R: 8, DOME BOX $125, BOTTLE UNKNOWN.

BLUE DENIM: KST, 1979, R: 6, MUNCHIES BAG $50, MATCHING STEEL/GLASS BOTTLE $35.

BLUE GINGHAM: AL, 1975, R: 6, BRUNCH BAG $50, MATCHING ROUND PLASTIC BOTTLE $35.

BLUE JEANS: KST, 1974, R: 6, MUNCHIES BAG $60, MATCHING STEEL/GLASS BOTTLE $35.

BOSTON RED SOX: AR, 1960s, R: 4, STANDARD BOX $120, STYROFOAM BOTTLE $10.

BOY ON ROCKET: UNK, 1960s, R: 8, STANDARD BOX $300, BOTTLE UNKNOWN.

BROWN: KST, 1972, R: 7, MUNCHIES BAG $50, MATCHING STEEL/GLASS BOTTLE $35.

BROWN (BOX-STYLE): AL, 1972, R: 7, BRUNCH BAG $50 STRIPED ROUND PLASTIC BOTTLE $25.

BROWN (DARK): UNK, 1970s, R: 5, BRUNCH BAG $175, STYROFOAM BOTTLE $10.

BROWN (LIGHT LEATHER): KST, 1960s, R: 6, MUNCHIES BAG $65, MATCHING STEEL/GLASS BOTTLE $25.

BUICK 1910: BV, 1974, R: 7, STANDARD BOX $135, STYROFOAM BOTTLE $10.

BULLWINKLE: AR, 1972, R: 10, BOX $2,000; STYROFOAM BOTTLE $10.

BULLWINKLE/TELSTAR THEME: TH, 1963; R: 9; BOX $600; BOTTLE $200.

CALICO: AL, 1980, R: 7, BRUNCH BAG $75, MATCHING ROUND PLASTIC BOTTLE $25.

CAN OF FLOWERS: AL, 1970s, R: 6, BRUNCH BAG $50, MATCHING ROUND PLASTIC BOTTLE $35.

CANDIES: KST, 1973, R: 7, MUNCHIES BAG $160, BOTTLE UNKNOWN.

CARE BEARS: ME, 1980s, R: 6, STANDARD BOX $75, BOTTLE UNKNOWN.

CARS: AR, 1960, R: 7, STANDARD BOX $145, STYROFOAM BOTTLE $10.

CHARLIE'S ANGELS: AL, 1978, R: 6, BRUNCH BAG $225, MATCHING ROUND PLASTIC BOTTLE $50.

CIRCUS: UNK, 1985, R: 7, SOFTY $55, BOTTLE UNKNOWN.

CIRCUS FUN: UNK, 1960s, R: 7, BOX $125, BOTTLE UNKNOWN.

COCA-COLA: AL, 1980, R: 7, STANDARD BOX $175, STYROFOAM BOTTLE $10.

COCA-COLA (BOX-STYLE): UNK, 1988, R: 8, BRUNCH BAG $65, BOTTLE UNKNOWN.

COLLEGE PENNANT: UNK, 1970s, R: 7, BRUNCH BAG $175, BOTTLE UNKNOWN.

CORSAGE: KST, 1970, R: 7, STANDARD BOX $165, MATCHING STEEL/GLASS BOTTLE $55.

CRAYON: UNK, 1984, R: 7, PUFFY $40, BOTTLE UNKNOWN.

DATE LINE (BEIGE or BLUE): HB, 1960s, R: 8, CUBE $155, BOTTLE UNKNOWN.

DATE LINE (BLUE or PINK): HB, 1960s, R: 8, STANDARD BOX $450, BOTTLE UNKNOWN.

DAWN : AL, 1971, R: 7, STANDARD BOX $145, MATCHING PLASTIC BOTTLE $40.

DAWN (GUITAR PLAYER): AL, 1971, R: 8, STANDARD BOX $145, MATCHING PLASTIC BOTTLE $40.

DEAR GOD KIDS: BB, 1986, R: 9, DOME BOX $85, BOTTLE UNKNOWN.

DEER: UNK, 1960s, R: 8, STANDARD BOX $255, BOTTLE UNKNOWN.

DENIM (& RED): UNK, R: 7, STANDARD BOX $45, BOTTLE UNKNOWN.

DENIM w/FLOWERS: UNK, 1984, R: 7, STANDARD BOX $35, BOTTLE UNKNOWN.

DIAGONAL: AL, 1974, R: 7, BRUNCH BAG $100, BOTTLE UNKNOWN.

DOG HOUSE: TB, 1974, R: 8, STANDARD BOX $125, MATCHING PLASTIC BOTTLE $45.

DOGGIE BAG: KST, 1978, R: 8, MUNCHIES BAG $170, BOTTLE UNKNOWN.

DONNY & MARIE (SHORT HAIR): AL, 1976, R: 6, STANDARD BOX $230, MATCHING PLASTIC BOTTLE $50.

DONNY & MARIE (SHORT HAIR): AL, 1978, R: 6, BRUNCH BAG $230, MATCHING ROUND PLASTIC BOTTLE $50.

DREAM BOAT: FE, 1960, R: 9, STANDARD BOX $850, STYROFOAM BOTTLE $10.

DUDLEY DO-RIGHT: AR, 1970s, R: 10, STANDARD BOX $2,000, STYROFOAM BOTTLE $10.

ENGINE CO. NO. 1: DA, 1974, R: 8, STANDARD BOX $125, BOTTLE UNKNOWN.

EUROPEAN MAP: UNK, R: 8, DOME BOX $250, BOTTLE UNKNOWN.

FAWN: UNK, 1960s, R: 8, STANDARD BOX $150, BOTTLE UNKNOWN.

FIRE DEPARTMENT: UNK, R: 8, SOFTY $115, BOTTLE UNKNOWN.

FISHING: AR, 1970, R: 9, STANDARD BOX $165, STYROFOAM BOTTLE $10.

FLYING NUN: ALADDIN, 1968; R: 6; BRUNCH BAG $175, BOTTLE $40.

FOOTBALL PLAYERS (TWO): AR, 1970s, R: 9, STANDARD BOX $155, STYROFOAM BOTTLE $10.

FREIHOFER'S COOKIES: UNK, 1960s, R: 9, STANDARD BOX $120, BOTTLE UNKNOWN.

GI JOE (AN AMERICAN HERO): KST, 1989, R: 6, ZIPPERED BAG $60, GENERIC PLASTIC BOTTLE $10.

GI JOE (COMBAT SOLDIER): MATTEL, UNK, R: 7, STANDARD BOX $375, STYROFOAM BOTTLE $10.

GADABOUT: AL, 1969, R: 8, BRUNCH BAG $125, MPB.

GADABOUT (BEIGE): AL, 1969, R: 7, BRUNCH BAG $115, MATCHING ROUND PLASTIC BOTTLE $45.

GADABOUT (PATTERN): AL, 1971, R: 7, BRUNCH BAG $125, MATCHING ROUND PLASTIC BOTTLE $45.

GARFIELD: ME, 1978, R: 7, STANDARD BOX $155, BOTTLE UNKNOWN.

GIRL & POODLE: AL, 1962, R: 8, STANDARD BOX $150, STYROFOAM BOTTLE $10.

GOAT BUTTE (BLACK or RED): AR, 1965, R: 9, STANDARD BOX $175, STYROFOAM BOTTLE $10.

GOODIE BOX: UNK, 1960, R: 8, STANDARD BOX $145, BOTTLE UNKNOWN.

GRAY: UNK, R: 8, DOME BOX $130, BOTTLE UNKNOWN.

Vinyl Boxes & Kits Not Pictured

GREEN w/GOLD BANDS: AL, 1968, R: 7, BRUNCH BAG $50, BOTTLE UNKNOWN.

HAPPY POWWOW: BV, 1970s, R: 9, STANDARD BOX $115, STYROFOAM BOTTLE $10.

HAUNTED HOUSE: DA, 1979, R: 8, STANDARD BOX $90, BOTTLE UNKNOWN.

HIGHWAY SIGNS: AV, 1988, R: 8, SNAP PACK $45, BOTTLE UNKNOWN.

HOLLY HOBBIE (ON BENCH): AL, 1978, R: 7, BRUNCH BAG $100, MATCHING ROUND PLASTIC BOTTLE $20.

INDIAN KIDS (CANADIAN): UNK, R: 9, DOME BOX $190, BOTTLE UNKNOWN.

JONATHAN LIVINGSTON SEAGULL: AL, 1974, R: 6, BRUNCH BAG $220, MATCHING ROUND PLASTIC BOTTLE $40.

JR. MISS SAFARI: PP, 1962, R: 7, PURSE-TYPE BAG $150, BOTTLE UNKNOWN.

JUNIOR DEB: AL, 1960 – 1962: R: 7, STANDARD BOX $270, MATCHING STEEL/GLASS BOTTLE $95.

KODAK GOLD: AL, 1970s, R: 7, ZIPPER BOX $90, MATCHING PLASTIC BOTTLE $25.

KODACOLOR II: AL, 1970s, R: 7, STANDARD BOX $100, MATCHING PLASTIC BOTTLE $25.

KRAZY DAISIES (BROWN OR GREEN): KST, 1970, R: 7, MUNCHIES BAG $65, MATCHING STEEL/GLASS BOTTLE $35.

LASSIE: AR, 1960s, R: 8, STANDARD BOX $125, STYROFOAM BOTTLE $10.

LEATHER DI: AL, 1965, R: 7, BRUNCH BAG $50, MATCHING STEEL/GLASS BOTTLE $35.

LIDDLE KIDDLES: KST, 1969, R: 8, STANDARD BOX $245, MATCHING STEEL/GLASS BOTTLE $65.

LIFESAVERS: UNK, 1970s, R: 7, TUBE-STYLE BAG $120, BOTTLE UNKNOWN.

LINUS! THE LIONHEARTED: AL, 1965, R: 9, STANDARD BOX $560, MATCHING STEEL/GLASS BOTTLE $115.

LION: BA, 1985, R: 7, PUFFY $60, BOTTLE UNKNOWN.

LION IN VAN: KST, 1978, R: 8, STANDARD BOX $150, BOTTLE UNKNOWN.

LIQUOR LABELS: UNK, R: 8, STANDARD BOX $325, BOTTLE UNKNOWN.

LITTLE BALLERINA: BV, 1975, R: 8, STANDARD BOX $100, STYROFOAM BOTTLE $10.

LOVE (LOGO): UNK, 1970s, R: 6, BRUNCH BAG $150, BOTTLE UNKNOWN.

LOVE (ONE GIRL): AL, 1975, R: 7, BRUNCH BAG $135, MATCHING ROUND PLASTIC BOTTLE $55.

LOVE (SIX KIDS): AL, 1972, R: 7, BRUNCH BAG $175, MATCHING ROUND PLASTIC BOTTLE $55.

LOVE (SIX KIDS): AL, 1972, R: 7, STANDARD BOX $165, MATCHING ROUND PLASTIC BOTTLE $50.

LOVE (THREE KIDS): AL, 1974, R: 7, BRUNCH BAG $140, MATCHING ROUND PLASTIC BOTTLE $55.

MARDI-GRAS: AL, 1971, R: 7, STANDARD BOX $85, MATCHING PLASTIC BOTTLE $30.

MARDI GRAS (a.k.a. PICADILLY) TALL OR SHORT: AL, 1970, R: 7, BRUNCH BAG $100, MATCHING ROUND PLASTIC BOTTLE $30.

MARY ANN: AL, 1960, R: 7, STANDARD BOX $80, MATCHING STEEL/GLASS BOTTLE $30.

MARY POPPINS: AL, 1966, R: 5, BRUNCH BAG $160, MATCHING STEEL/GLASS BOTTLE $85.

MEDALLION: AL, 1965, R: 6, BRUNCH BAG $220, MATCHING STEEL/GLASS BOTTLE $85.

MICKEY MOUSE: ME, UNK, R: 8, STANDARD BOX $135, BOTTLE UNKNOWN.

MOD MISS (BLACK): AL, 1971, R: 7, BRUNCH BAG $145, BOTTLE UNKNOWN.

MONKEES: KST, 1967, R: 8, STANDARD BOX $425, MATCHING STEEL/GLASS BOTTLE $125.

MR. PEANUT: DA, 1979, R: 8, SNAP PACK $115, BOTTLE UNKNOWN.

MUSHROOMS (TAN): AL, 1973, R: 7, BRUNCH BAG $135, MATCHING ROUND PLASTIC BOTTLE $45.

MY COOKIE CARRIER (POSSIBLY SAFEWAY): UNK, R: 8, STANDARD BOX $85, BOTTLE UNKNOWN.

NEW ZOO REVUE: AL, 1970s, R: 8, STANDARD BOX $220, MATCHING PLASTIC BOTTLE $60.

NICKELODEON: UNK, R: 7, STANDARD BOX $100, BOTTLE UNKNOWN.

OGILVY & MATHER: UNK, R: 9, STANDARD BOX $65, BOTTLE UNKNOWN.

ORANGE SWIRL: AL, 1965, R: 7, BRUNCH BAG $225, BOTTLE UNKNOWN.

OUR SONG: UNK, 1960s, R: 8, STANDARD BOX $255, BOTTLE UNKNOWN.

PAC-MAN: AL, 1985, R: 7, PUFFY $70, BOTTLE UNKNOWN.

PATCHES (a.k.a. DENIM): TALL OR SHORT, KST, 1972, R: 7, MUNCHIES BAG $65, MATCHING STEEL/GLASS BOTTLE $35, GENERIC PLASTIC BOTTLE $20.

PENELOPE & PENNY: GA, 1970s, R: 8, STANDARD BOX $125, STYROFOAM BOTTLE $10.

PETER PAN PEANUT BUTTER: UNK, R: 8, CUBE $130, BOTTLE UNKNOWN.

PICADILLY: AL, 1971, R: 6, STANDARD BOX $95, MATCHING ROUND PLASTIC BOTTLE $35.

PICADILLY GREEN (a.k.a. MARDI GRAS): AL, 1971, R: 7, BRUNCH BAG $100, MATCHING ROUND PLASTIC BOTTLE $35.

PIQUE: ME, 1985, R: 8, STANDARD BOX $130, BOTTLE UNKNOWN.

PLAID (TARTAN): AL, 1962, R: 7, BRUNCH BAG $75, MATCHING STEEL/GLASS BOTTLE $25.

PLAID (TARTAN): AL, 1970, R: 7, BRUNCH BAG $75, MATCHING ROUND PLASTIC BOTTLE $20.

PONYTAIL (STRAP HANDLE): KST, 1960, R: 8, STANDARD BOX $190, MATCHING STEEL/GLASS BOTTLE $55.

PONYTAIL w/GRAY BORDER: KST, 1960s, R: 9, STANDARD BOX $230, MATCHING STEEL/GLASS BOTTLE $55.

PONYTAIL: KST, 1965, R: 8, STANDARD BOX WITH FRONT FLAP $460, MATCHING STEEL/GLASS BOTTLE $55.

PONYTAIL TID-BIT KIT (STRAP HANDLE): KST, 1962, R: 8, STANDARD BOX $235, MATCHING STEEL/GLASS BOTTLE $55.

PRINCESS: AL, 1962, R: 7, BRUNCH BAG $155, MATCHING STEEL/GLASS BOTTLE $65.

PSYCHEDELIC (BLUE): KST, 1968, R: 7, TALL MUNCHIES BAG $100, MATCHING STEEL/GLASS BOTTLE $65.

PSYCHEDELIC (YELLOW): KST, 1960s, R: 7, PURSE-TYPE BAG $135, BOTTLE UNKNOWN.

PSYCHEDELIC (YELLOW): AL, 1970, R: 7, BRUNCH BAG $175, BLACK & YELLOW PLASTIC $90.

PUSSYCATS: AL, 1968, R: 8, BRUNCH BAG $250, MATCHING ROUND PLASTIC BOTTLE $75.

QUILT WORK: UNK, R: 8, DOME BOX $150, BOTTLE UNKNOWN.

RACE CAR: UNK, R: 8, PUFFY $50, BOTTLE UNKNOWN.

RED (PLAIN, SOLID COLOR): KST, 1960s, R: 8, DOME BOX $130, MATCHING STEEL/GLASS BOTTLE $30.

RED FLOWER (a.k.a. CAN OF FLOWERS w/GOLF BALL): AL, 1970s, R: 7, BRUNCH BAG $50, MATCHING ROUND PLASTIC BOTTLE $35.

RED FLOWER w/TENNIS RACQUET: AL, 1970s, R: 7, BRUNCH BAG $85, MATCHING ROUND PLASTIC BOTTLE $35.

RED PLAID (DIAGONAL): UNK, 1970s, R: 7, BRUNCH BAG $115, BOTTLE UNKNOWN.

RED ROSES (TALL): KST, 1968, R: 7, MUNCHIES BAG $100, MATCHING STEEL/GLASS BOTTLE $65.

RED ROSES (SHORT): KST, 1970, R: 7, MUNCHIES BAG $100, MATCHING STEEL/GLASS BOTTLE $85.

RINGLING BROS. & BARNUM: UNK, 1980s, R: 8, STANDARD BOX $110, BOTTLE UNKNOWN.

ROAD TOTE (RED or YELLOW): UNK, R: 8, DOME BOX $230, BOTTLE UNKNOWN.

ROY ROGERS (CREAM): KST, 1960, R: 9, STANDARD BOX $700, SAME BOTTLE AS #297 BUT WITH YELLOW SKY.

SNOOPY: KST, 1988, R: 7, SOFTY $50, BOTTLE UNKNOWN.

SNOW WHITE: UNK, 1967, R: 9, PURSE-TYPE BAG $300, BOTTLE UNKNOWN.

SNOW WHITE: AL, 1975, R: 8, STANDARD BOX $225, MATCHING PLASTIC BOTTLE $50.

SODA: UNK, 1960s, R: 7, STANDARD BOX $160, BOTTLE UNKNOWN.

SOUPY SALES: KST, 1966, R: 9, STANDARD BOX $495, BOTTLE UNKNOWN.

SPEEDY PETEY & PALS: GA, UNK, R: 8, STANDARD BOX $150, BOTTLE UNKNOWN.

SPEEDY TURTLE; KST, 1978, R: 8, DRAWSTRING BAG $185, BOTTLE UNKNOWN.

SQUARES (BLUE OR WHITE): UNK, R: 7, STANDARD BOX $65, BOTTLE UNKNOWN.

STALLIONS: AL, 1962, R: 8, BRUNCH BAG 200, MATCHING STEEL/GLASS BOTTLE $35.

STARDOME LUNCH BUNCH: UNK, R: 9, STANDARD BOX $55, BOTTLE UNKNOWN.

STRAWBERRIES: AL, 1970s, R: 7, BRUNCH BAG $50, MATCHING ROUND PLASTIC BOTTLE $35.

SUNSET: DA, 1979, R: 8, SNAP PACK $65, BOTTLE UNKNOWN.

SWEETER DAYS: KST, 1973, R: 8, MUNCHIES BAG $150, BOTTLE UNKNOWN.

TAN (PLAIN BROWN w/DARK RIM): UNK, R: 8, DOME BOX $125, BOTTLE UNKNOWN.

TARTAN — SEE PLAID

TENNIS MOTIF: AL, 1976, R: 8, BRUNCH BAG $200, MATCHING ROUND PLASTIC BOTTLE $40.

TIGER w/UMBRELLA: NE, R: 9, STANDARD BOX $150, STYROFOAM BOTTLE $10.

TOWN & COUNTRY (TALL): AL, 1965, R: 7, BRUNCH BAG $65, MATCHING STEEL/GLASS BOTTLE $40.

TOWN & COUNTRY (SHORT): AL, 1968, R: 7, BRUNCH BAG $65, MATCHING STEEL/GLASS BOTTLE $40.

TRANS-FORMERS, THE MOVIE: UNK, 1989, R: 7, STANDARD BOX $95, BOTTLE UNKNOWN.

TWEED: UNK, R: 8, STANDARD BOX $65, BOTTLE UNKNOWN.

TWIGGY: AL, 1967, R: 8, BRUNCH BAG $265, MATCHING STEEL/GLASS BOTTLE $125.

U.S. MAIL: AL, 1967, R: 8, BRUNCH BAG $185, MATCHING ROUND PLASTIC BOTTLE $50.

UNIVERSAL SPORTS KIT (a.k.a. "NATIONAL OPEN"): UN, 1960s, R: 8, STANDARD BOX w/STRAP HANDLE $440, MATCHING STEEL/GLASS BOTTLE $160.

WASHINGTON APPLE: UNK, R: 8, STANDARD BOX $35, BOTTLE UNKNOWN.

WHITE DOTS: AL, 1969, R: 8, BRUNCH BAG $55, MATCHING ROUND PLASTIC BOTTLE $45.

WHITE PSYCHEDELIC: KST, 1962, R: 9, STANDARD BOX $320, BOTTLE UNKNOWN.

WISE GUY: KST, 1977, R: 8, MUNCHIES BAG $150, BOTTLE UNKNOWN.

WIZARD IN VAN: KST, 1978, R: 9, STANDARD BOX $155, BOTTLE UNKNOWN.

WONDER WOMAN (YELLOW): AL, 1978, R: 6, STANDARD BOX $220, MATCHING ROUND PLASTIC BOTTLE $45.

WORLD TRAVELER: AL, 1961, R: 8, BRUNCH BAG $160, BOTTLE UNKNOWN.

WRANGLER: AL, 1962, R: 8, STANDARD BOX $335, MATCHING STEEL/GLASS BOTTLE $125.

YELLOW (SOLID COLOR, STRAP HANDLE): UNK, R: 8, PURSE-TYPE BOX $35, NO BOTTLE MADE.

YOGI BEAR: AL, 1970s, R: 8; STANDARD BOX $450, NO BOTTLE MADE.

495. front

496. front & bottle

495. BATMAN				
KST	1989	R: 5	STANDARD BOX $15	MATCHING ROUND PLASTIC BOTTLE $10

496. THE CALIFORNIA RAISINS				
KST	1987	R: 6	STANDARD BOX $10	MATCHING ROUND PLASTIC BOTTLE $5

 497. front

497. COCA-COLA				
AL	1981	R: 6	STANDARD BOX $20	MATCHING ROUND PLASTIC BOTTLE $15

498. front

499. front

498. CRAZY SHIRT				
UNI	1983	R: 5	DOME BOX $25	BOTTLE UNKNOWN

499. CREATURE FEATURES MONSTER BOX				
PAM & FRANK U.S.A. MADE IN CHINA	1990s	R: 6	BOX $15	NO BOTTLE MADE

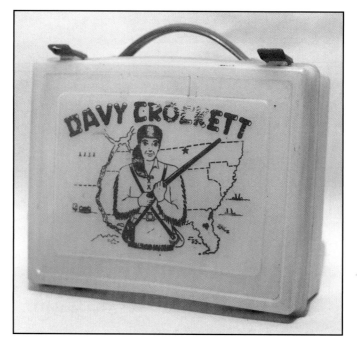

500. front

500. DAVY CROCKETT				
UNK	UNK	R: 10	STANDARD BOX $500	BOTTLE UNKNOWN

501. front & bottle

502. front

501. FISHER PRICE RED BARN MINI TOY LUNCH KIT				
FP	1962	R: 6	MINI DOME BOX $10	MATCHING ROUND PLASTIC BOTTLE $10

502. FLINTSTONES				
KST	©1977	R: 6	STANDARD BOX $30	MATCHING PLASTIC BOTTLE $15

503. front

503. FLINTSTONES				
KST	1981	R: 7	DOME BOX $40	MATCHING ROUND PLASTIC BOTTLE $15

504. front

505. front & bottle

504. HELLO KITTY				
SANRIO	1990s	R: 6	STANDARD BOX $15	BOTTLE UNKNOWN

505. JETSONS (THE MOVIE)				
AL	1990	R: 7	STANDARD BOX $15	MATCHING ROUND PLASTIC BOTTLE $5

506. front

506. LUNCH EXPRESS				
TAIWAN	UNK	R: 5	BOX $10	BOTTLE UNKNOWN

507. front

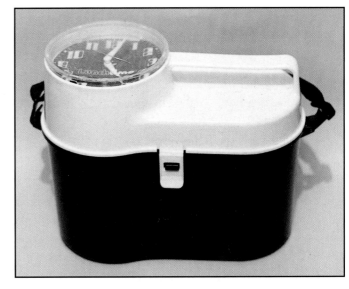

508. front

507. LUNCH MAN RADIO LUNCHBOX				
FD	1986	R: 7	BOX $20	BOTTLE UNKNOWN

508. LUNCH TIME CLOCK LUNCHBOX				
MK	1988	R: 7	BOX $20	MATCHING ROUND PLASTIC BOTTLE $10

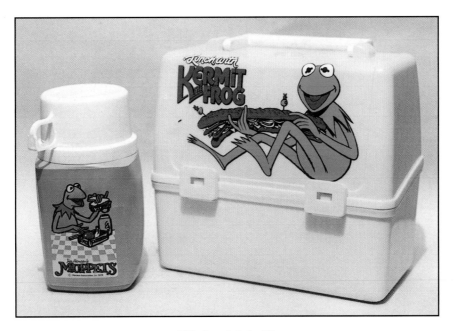

509. front & bottle

509. LUNCH WITH KERMIT THE FROG				
KST	1988	R: 6	DOME BOX $20	MATCHING ROUND PLASTIC BOTTLE $20

510. front

510. back

510. MICKEY MOUSE			
SELANDIA DESIGNS TAIWAN	R: 6	STANDARD BOX $35	MATCHING ROUND PLASTIC BOTTLE $15

511a. front & bottle

511b. front & bottle

511a. MICKEY MOUSE				
AL	1989	R: 6	BOX $15	MATCHING ROUND PLASTIC BOTTLE $10

511b. MINNIE MOUSE				
AL	1989	R: 7	BOX $15	MATCHING ROUND PLASTIC BOTTLE $10

512. front & bottle

512. MIGHTY MOUSE				
KST	1979	R: 8	STANDARD BOX $125	MATCHING SQUARE PLASTIC BOTTLE $50

513. front

514. front

513. MY LITTLE PONY				
HASBRO UK	1984	R: 4	STANDARD BOX $10	BOTTLE UNKNOWN

514. 90210				
KST	1991	R: 6	BOX $15	BOTTLE UNKNOWN

515. front

515. POOH'S HOUSE				
UNK	UNK	R: 7	BOX $10	BOTTLE UNKNOWN

516. front

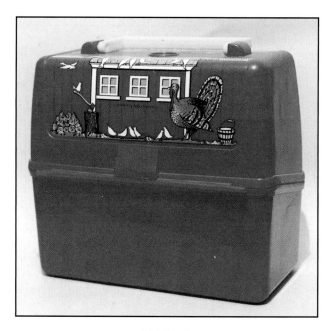

516. back

516. RED BARN				
KST	1982	R: 6	DOME BOX $15	MATCHING SQUARE PLASTIC BOTTLE $15

517. front & bottle

517. ROCKY & BULLWINKLE AT FROSTBITE FALLS				
KST	1991	R: 9	STANDARD BOX $150	MATCHING ROUND PLASTIC BOTTLE $25

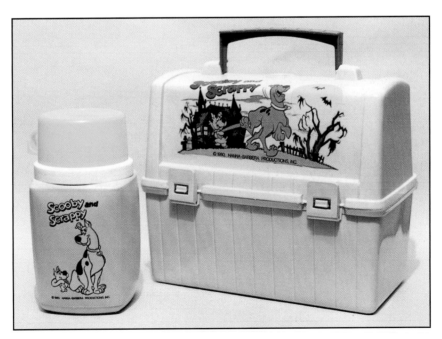

518. front & bottle

518. SCOOBY & SCRAPPY				
KST	1980	R: 7	DOME BOX $50	MATCHING ROUND PLASTIC BOTTLE $10

519. front

520. front

			519. ST. LOUIS CARDINALS (GATORADE)	
TA	1990s	R: 5	STANDARD BOX $20	BOTTLE UNKNOWN

			520. STYROFOAM LUNCHBOX	
UNK	1980	R: 7	BOX $15	HANDLE SAYS "DIVAJEX, TUSTIN CA"

521. bottle

		521. SWEET HONESTY PERFUME IN MINI THERMOS BOTTLE	
AVON	1980s	R: 3	ROUND PLASTIC BOTTLE $5

REPRODUCTION LUNCHBOXES

Known reproductions of classic boxes are being made in China for G-Whiz, an American company in Van Nuys, California. It is very easy to tell the reproductions from the originals — G-Whiz is stamped on the backs of the new boxes. There are also differences in the clasps, hinges, and handles. The new boxes are also lighter in weight than the old ones.

G-Whiz has made 10 or 15 classic boxes, including Campus Queen, Captain Astro, Fireball XL5, Green Hornet, Lone Ranger ('54 red band), and Lost in Space. They have also made a really cool new X-Files box.

 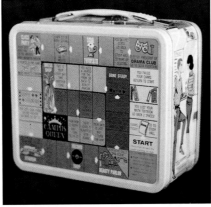 

Campus Queen, standard box, $13.50.

The Green Hornet, standard box, $13.50.

Lost in Space, dome box, $17.00.
Thanks to Haggis McBaggis of Portland, OR, for G-Whiz information.

GLOSSARY

Back: With the clasp facing forward, the reverse side of the lunchbox.

Band: The continuous flat metal strip that joins the front and back of the box; refers to the north, south, east, and west sides.

Body: The industry name for the band; sometimes called the saddle.

Bottom: An industry name for the back of the box; does not refer to the base on which the box sits.

Brunch Bag: What Aladdin called their tall, oval vinyl bags with zippered lids and strap handles.

Cap: The thermos bottle stopper, made of cork or plastic.

Carry-all: An oval or rectangular lunchbox with one or two moveable metal strap-like handles.

Cup: The metal or plastic drinking vessel which fits over the top of a thermos bottle.

Decal: A clear sheet with an illustration on the front and adhesive on the back.

Dome Box: A rectangular box with a rounded lid, two latches on the front, and the handle on top.

Drawstring Bag: A vinyl lunch bag with a metal base box inside and sides that close at the top with a vinyl drawstring.

Embossed Box: A box with the art stamped in relief, raising it from the surface of the box.

Face: The industry name for the front side of the box.

Flat Box: A box with the art lithographed on the surface of the box.

Front: The common name for the face of the box.

Holtemp: Generic American Thermos Company bottle of the 1950s.

Kit: A lunchbox and thermos bottle.

Licensed Character Lunchbox: A box with a registered TV, movie, toy or game illustration. The licensee pays a royalty to the licensor on every kit sold.

Lithography: The printing process used to print four-color illustrations on metal, paper or vinyl sheets.

Munchies Bag: KST's name for their tall, oval vinyl bags with zippered lids and strap handles.

Pail: Another name for older lunchboxes.

Rim: The edges of the lunchbox, front and back.

Sleeve: The body of a thermos bottle; the round steel tube into which the glass liner was inserted.

Softies: Aladdin's name for their flat, standard vinyl boxes.

Standard Box: A rectangular, flat-sided "suitcase style" lunchbox of metal, plastic or vinyl — the most common and plentiful box made.

Thermos Bottle: Although the name is trademarked by the American Thermos Bottle Company (later King Seely Thermos), thermos has become the household name for the vacuum bottle.

BIBLIOGRAPHY

Aikens, Larry, *Pictorial Price Guide to Metal Lunchboxes & Thermoses*, L-W Book Sales, Gas City, IN, Revised Edition, 1999.

Aikens, Larry, *Pictorial Price Guide to Vinyl & Plastic Lunchboxes & Thermoses*, L-W Book Sales, Gas City, IN, Revised Edition, 1995.

Bruce, Scott, *The Fifties and Sixties Lunchbox*, Chronicle Books, San Francisco, 1988.

Bruce, Scott, *The Official Price Guide to Lunchbox Collectibles*, House of Collectibles, New York, 1989.

Congdon-Martin, Douglas, *Tobacco Tins — A Collector's Guide*, Schiffer Publishing, Ltd., Atglen, PA 1992.

Persinger, Ralph, *The Paileontologist's Retort Newsletter*, Mr. LunchBox Publications, March-April 1992, May-June 1992, July-August 1992.

Research Federation Forum, *On the Cusp — and Over: A Look at Generational Differences*, Newspaper Association of America, Vienna, VA, July/August 1999.

Weatherman, Hazel Marie, *Colored Glassware of the Depression Era 2*, Weatherman Glassbooks, Springfield, MO, 1974.

Woodall, Allen and Sean Brickell, *The Illustrated Encyclopedia of Metal Lunchboxes*, Schiffer Publications, Ltd., West Chester, PA, 1992.

INDEX

Index

Index

Index

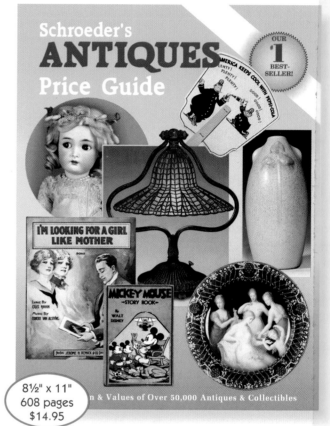